Planning Effectively for Educational Quality

An Outcomes-Based
Approach for Colleges
Committed to Excellence

William H. Bergquist

Jack L. Armstrong

Planning Effectively
for Educational Quality

PUBLISHED IN COOPERATION WITH
THE COUNCIL OF INDEPENDENT COLLEGES

Jossey-Bass Publishers

San Francisco • London • 1986

PLANNING EFFECTIVELY FOR EDUCATIONAL QUALITY
An Outcomes-Based Approach for Colleges Committed to Excellence
by William H. Bergquist and Jack L. Armstrong

Copyright © 1986 by: Council of Independent Colleges
One Dupont Circle
Washington, D.C. 20036

Jossey-Bass Inc., Publishers
433 California Street
San Francisco, California 94104

Jossey-Bass Limited
28 Banner Street
London EC1Y 8QE

Library of Congress Cataloging-in-Publication Data

Bergquist, William H.
    Planning effectively for educational quality.

    (The Jossey-Bass higher education series)
    "Published in cooperation with the Council of
Independent Colleges."
    Bibliography: p. 205
    Includes index.
    1. Education, Higher—United States—Aims and
objectives.   2. Educational planning—United States.
I. Armstrong, Jack L.   II. Title.   III. Series.
LA227.3.B48   1986   378'.107   86–45620
ISBN 1-55542-017-6

Manufactured in the United States of America

The paper in this book meets the guidelines for
permanence and durability of the Committee on
Production Guidelines for Book Longevity of the
Council on Library Resources.

JACKET DESIGN BY WILLI BAUM

FIRST EDITION

Code 8649

The Jossey-Bass
Higher Education Series

Contents

**Part Three: Reviewing the Success
of the Planning Model**

Preface

During a week's vacation at the beach, Gene Cooper struggles to compose a position paper on the liberal arts and general education to present to the faculty at Sanders College. As the dean of this college for the past three years, Cooper wants to encourage new perspectives on the old, enduring issues of the nature and value of a high-quality liberal arts education. What characteristics enable a graduating student to make it through this complex, demanding world with a modicum of civility and with a record of achievement in service to his or her fellow citizens? What role should the college play in fostering the development of these qualities?

At Northstar Community College, the faculty recently voted to introduce an interdisciplinary course on "Society and Its Values." Members of the teaching team now face the task of planning a section of the course called "Conflict Surrounding the War in Vietnam." The faculty must define what they want to accomplish in this section of the course. Are members of the teaching team clear about their own values and the type of student they wish this section of the course to produce? Do they simply want the students to learn about the war, or are there certain values they want the students to embrace at the end of this section? Is it even appropriate for Northstar Community College to inculcate values, or should the college serve only as a forum for introducing value-related issues? Or is it possible for the faculty to help students clarify their own values?

Susan Harkovine teaches Introduction to Biology at North-eastern State University. Most of the students in this course are enrolled in the prenursing program; some of the students are in the premed program, but there are only a few biology majors. Susan ponders what she really wants to achieve in this course and how she will know whether she has successfully met the needs of her students and her university. How can she redesign this course to have an impact on the lives and professions of her students? Or is it presumptuous to want this course to contribute to making students better nurses or doctors? And yet, when Susan looks at the time available for her to plan for this course and at the large number of students enrolled and their seeming lack of motivation, she wonders whether she should lower her expectations for both this course and her students.

Dean Cooper, the teaching team at Northstar College, and Susan Harkovine are all struggling with the increasingly important issue of quality in higher education. Colleges and universities today are being scrutinized to determine whether they adequately meet the pressing and changing needs of society and the nation. In addition to these concerns, the decline in numbers of traditional students and in the availability of resources—material and financial—affects all colleges and universities.

We believe that the key to meeting social and national educational needs and to living successfully with limited resources during the current and coming decades is to be found in offering high-quality educational services for the individual student. Only those institutions that can demonstrate quality in their offerings to students will hold a competitive edge in the ongoing struggle to thrive, as well as survive, in the turbulent years ahead.

This observation is, of course, not unique to us. What we offer in this book that is of unique value to colleagues in academic institutions is a blueprint for achieving quality. Specifically, we provide a detailed planning model for selecting, designing, testing, and implementing an academic program of highest quality.

This planning model was developed in conjunction with

a major curriculum development effort that involved sixty liberal arts colleges in the United States. However, because of our own personal experiences in larger, state-supported institutions and the general nature of the planning model itself, we have written this book with a much larger audience in mind. University professors, community college deans, and department chairs in state universities will all find valuable guidelines, techniques, and procedures in this book. The planning model we offer is distinctive, not only because it is practical and detailed, but also because it is anchored in the process of defining student learning outcomes and in student development theory and research. We firmly believe that a college or university faculty member or an academic administrator who reviews with some care the concepts introduced in this book will find at least one new and better way of working toward educational quality.

Background on Project QUE

By the late 1970s, the member presidents of the Council of Independent Colleges (CIC) were well aware that the continuing vitality of independent colleges during the 1980s would be directly tied to their ability to provide a high-quality education for undergraduate students of all ages. At the same time, these college leaders came to doubt the conventional wisdom of defining quality primarily in terms of educational inputs (human and financial resources). Many presidents and deans came to believe that assessments of educational quality should give major consideration to the result of education, to the impact the educational experience actually has on students. With this concern for enhancing educational quality and an expanded view of the nature of quality, the CIC board of directors embarked on a special multiyear program to assist member colleges in sustaining and advancing the quality of their undergraduate programs.

The initial CIC effort—the Project on Quality Undergraduate Education (Project QUE)—was a four-year (1980–1984), $2 million program, funded by the W. K. Kellogg Foundation. It enabled each of sixty member colleges to design and implement a single academic program, one based on human development principles and student learning outcomes. Participation in Project QUE was based on competitive proposals. Participating colleges received a detailed project work manual (Bergquist and Armstrong, 1985) describing the Academic Planning Model that is presented in this book and took an active part in regional workshops, campus consultations, intensive professional development seminars for faculty and academic administrators, and three national institutes.

Three major assumptions helped to define the purposes of Project QUE:

1. If collegiate institutions are to survive and thrive in the 1990s, they must do more than secure sufficient financial resources and student enrollments. Each institution must organize and use its human resources effectively to provide high-quality educational services dedicated to the growth and development of the individual student. This is the key to the future of collegiate institutions.

2. Conventional wisdom concerning what constitutes "high-quality education" will not be appropriate for most institutions in the 1990s. Although traditional emphasis on quantifiable criteria continues to be important (for example, entering student test scores, number of volumes in the library, low faculty-student ratio, high proportion of faculty with terminal degrees), the central focus in defining and achieving "high quality" must be on the educational process. This requires serious attention to be given to what actually happens to promote (and inhibit) the cognitive and affective development of the individual student through the educational program.

3. An institution's general reputation for high quality can often be traced to a small number of academic programs done well over time. Thus, an institution seeking to improve its general reputation during the 1990s should concentrate on those few academic programs that hold the greatest promise for promoting the growth and development of the individual student.

Project QUE yielded many immediate benefits for the participating colleges, but its greatest benefit may come from the opportunity to test and refine a comprehensive academic planning model that is specifically designed to enhance the quality of contemporary collegiate programs. It is to this model that we turn our attention in this book.

Overview of the Contents

Planning Effectively for Educational Quality consists of three parts. Part One discusses the standards by which quality can be measured and presents the concept behind the planning model described in this book. Chapter One provides the reader with a set of seven criteria for defining quality in an educational institution. Chapter Two offers a rationale for the planning model, emphasizing in particular the value of a cyclical mode of planning that encourages both reflection and action and the important differences to be observed when moving between the domains of information, values, and ideas in any planning process.

The planning model is fully described in Part Two. Chapter Three concerns the selection of a target program for quality development, while Chapter Four focuses on the tools and procedures involved in identifying the student learning outcomes that serve as the basis for this target program. In Chapter Five, the reader is provided with a set of steps for designing an ideal and then a realistic program that meets the identified outcomes. Chapter Six offers perhaps the most distinctive portion of the planning model: a variety of methods for pilot testing the newly designed program and for evaluating these tests and making the necessary refinements so that the program will be maximally effective when first implemented. Chapter Seven discusses full-scale implementation of the program.

Chapter Eight, which constitutes Part Three, explores the larger questions of academic planning, institutional leadership, interinstitutional cooperation, and the role of student learning outcomes in postsecondary education.

Throughout the book we have tried to avoid generalities

and obscure educational terminology. Where appropriate, we have anchored our discussions and descriptions with case studies and illustrative examples from one or more of the sixty colleges involved in Project QUE. At times, we have also offered examples from colleges or universities that did not participate. These institutions are not identified because they did not at the time know of or necessarily wish to participate in a study of academic planning.

The programs that have been developed according to the model we describe here illustrate its applicability to many types of colleges and to many kinds and levels of academic programs: single courses, new degrees, programs for particular groups of students (freshmen, older students, majors, and so on), and campuswide programs.

Although certain sequential steps are recommended, the reader will find that the colleges that have already used this planning model developed many variations on these steps. The heart of this planning model is a set of principles and concepts: consensual agreement on educational programs to be newly developed or strengthened, the specification of student learning outcomes, the importance of student development perspectives, the value of an ideal design, the role of both formative and summative evaluation, and the critical importance of pilot testing. Specific steps and timetables have to be altered to fit each institution, but we believe that adherence to the fundamental concepts in each phase can significantly influence the selection and development of educational programs of high quality.

The Academic Planning Model is designed as a four-year program. Particular situations, however, may demand or facilitate a more rapid pace. However, we would caution against hasty decisions and precipitous program development. In recent years, "necessity" has too often been used to rationalize expediency, resulting in programs of lesser quality than students deserve. When the quality of a program is not in the best interest of the student, we believe it is not in the best interest of the institution either.

In this book we have provided sufficient description of the processes, procedures, and planning tools to enable a college or university planning team to successfully develop high-quality educational programs. This task requires both reflection and action. It requires a flexible yet systematic use of information, values, and ideas. We should and can expect no less of our academic planning efforts.

Acknowledgments

A project as large and complex as Project QUE owes its life and character to many people working in a variety of capacities on individual campuses and in the national office. We would like to thank each of the campus coordinators for their efforts. Many of their names are listed in Appendix A. We would also like to express our appreciation to the presidents and academic deans at the participating colleges who provided ample and enthusiastic support for their campus projects. We speak often of the valuable role played by these men and women. The many faculty members and academic administrators who participated in planning and implementing new or revised academic programs through Project QUE deserve considerable credit for the success of this project, as do the students who have lived with these experiments and have, in many instances, helped to plan the programs.

Our sincere thanks also go to the W. K. Kellogg Foundation for its generous support of both Project QUE and the preparation of this volume. In particular we wish to acknowledge the role played by Peter Ellis and, at an earlier point, George Hansen. The Kellogg Foundation has consistently been at the forefront of innovation in American higher education and has always fostered a special respect for the welfare of students and for the communities in which students live and to which they return.

Our special gratitude is extended to our friend and colleague Gary Quehl, past president of the Council of Independent Colleges. During more than a decade of leadership in this organization, Gary Quehl was a major source of new ideas and a supporter of other people's ideas. Rarely has a leader in American higher education been so willing to promote success and excellence rather than merely avoid failure. Other members of the CIC staff were equally supportive and provided competent assistance: Mary Glenzenski, Marianne Bosworth, and Lucy Race. Nancy Mosier's effective administration of Project QUE was of particular value.

We wish to express our appreciation to several of our colleagues who provided generous assistance in the preparation of specific chapters of this book, as well as assistance throughout the project. Chapter One owes much to the insights of Elinor Greenberg, a major contributor to the original questions concerning quality for Project QUE. The work of Steven Phillips is evident throughout the second and third chapters, as is the work of Jack Lindquist. The remaining chapters have benefited greatly from the practical experience and insights of Ronald Crossley. We thank each of these people for their assistance and hope that we have done justice to their ideas and warrant their unfailing support.

Jerry Gaff was continually available for a valuable sharing of experiences and exchange of ideas, despite his busy schedule as director of another national project coincident with Project QUE. Joanne Kurfiss provided her special expertise on both the theory of and research on student development. As special consultants to Project QUE and to the participating colleges and as frequent workshop leaders, many others contributed to the evolution of Project QUE, to the development of this book, and to our own thinking, enthusiasm, and professional growth.

Finally, we wish to express our appreciation to our wives, Kathleen O'Donnell and Barbara Share, who have been exceptional sources of support and encouragement throughout this project. Both of these women have had considerable experience in higher education; as a result, their ideas as well as their support have been central to the preparation of this book.

October 1986

William H. Bergquist
Walnut Creek, California

Jack L. Armstrong
Machias, Maine

The Authors

William H. Bergquist is president of the Professional School of Psychology in San Francisco, California. He received his B.A. degree (1958) at Occidental College in Los Angeles, California, and his M.A. (1963) and Ph.D. (1969) degrees at the University of Oregon at Eugene, all in psychology. Bergquist's major areas of research and consultation include organization development, institutional planning, and professional development. He is currently conducting research on the organizational culture in federal prisons and on the developmental stages of couples.

Bergquist served as architect and major consultant to the Project on Quality Undergraduate Education of the Council of Independent Colleges and as chief consultant with this national organization from 1975 to 1983. Over the past fifteen years, he has provided consultation and training to faculty and administrators from four hundred colleges and universities in the United States and Canada. In addition, Bergquist has co-authored or coedited more than thirty books and articles, including *Designing Undergraduate Education* (1981), *A Handbook for Faculty Development*, Vols. 1 (1975), 2 (1977), and 3 (1981), *Developing the College Curriculum* (1977), and *A Comprehensive Approach to Institutional Development* (1976).

Jack L. Armstrong is vice-president and dean of academic affairs at the University of Maine at Machias. He received his B.A. degree (1958) from William Jewell College in biology, his M.Ed. degree (1959) from the University of Illinois in counseling, and his Ph.D. degree (1964) from the University of Minnesota in educational psychology and psychology.

Prior to serving as executive director of the Project on Quality Undergraduate Education of the Council of Independent Colleges, Armstrong served as a department chair at Waynesburg College, an associate dean and dean at Macalester College, and president of Bradford College. At each institution he was also a member of the psychology faculty. While at Macalester College, he served as the first coordinator of the consortium of St. Paul colleges. He has published articles and consulted for colleges throughout the country on general education, curriculum development, and interinstitutional cooperation.

※※※※※※※※※※

Planning Effectively for Educational Quality

*An Outcomes-Based
Approach for Colleges
Committed to Excellence*

ༀༀༀༀ 1 ༀༀༀༀ

Seven Criteria
for a High-Quality
Academic Program

Indicators of High Quality

In higher education, as in many other institutions in our society, we have tended to look at quantitative ''input'' indicators to identify and assess what we mean by high quality. Our criteria often answer the questions ''How many?'' and ''How much?'' For example: ''How many volumes are there in the library?'' ''How many faculty members have doctorates?'' ''How many research projects and publications have been produced?'' ''How many students come from the upper quarter of their high school graduating class?'' ''How many minority students were admitted?'' ''How much is the endowment portfolio worth?''

These quantitative measures are important. They provide descriptions that give us a profile or outline of an institution. But they do not tell the whole story. While traditional, quantitative indicators offer a particular perspective on any one of our colleges and universities—its scope, capability, and resources— they tell us little about the institution in terms of either the ''output'' of the college or university or what actually occurs within the institution with regard to the process of education.

Output-oriented measures of quality typically focus on the characteristics of students as they graduate from the institution or on their level of success as they enter various phases of their postcollegiate careers. Output measures taken at graduation may focus on specific student competencies (such as critical

1

thinking, expressive writing, or persuasive oral communication) or on levels of student achievement on standard academic measures (such as the Graduate Record Examination). Postgraduate measures might include rate of admission to graduate school, percentage of job placements within six months after graduation, average level of income five years after graduation, or even percentage of graduates who are listed in *Who's Who in America.*

While these measures often give a sense of the relative status enjoyed by a particular college or university and provide a strong recruitment tool for new students, measures of output, in isolation, provide very little useful information regarding the true quality of the programs being offered by the college or university. Are graduates of the college or university successful because of the programs in which they were enrolled, or did they enter the institution already possessing the skills, knowledge, and contacts that they would later use to advance their own careers? Are the characteristics of graduates produced by the educational programs at this school, or did students at this institution acquire these characteristics before enrolling in the school or in other ways while enrolled (extracurricular activities)? The quality of an educational program can be adequately assessed only if one can determine the extent to which the program has directly contributed to the desired outcome. This is called the "value-added" definition of quality. To the extent that this college or university has added value to the student, in terms of desired characteristics, desired skills, or desired life or career outcomes, and to the extent that the college or university can specify the way(s) in which it has contributed this value, to that extent it can be described as offering educational quality.

Ultimately, of course, the quality of an educational program will be defined by input, output, *and* value-added measures, assessed in interrelationship with one another. A comprehensive definition of educational value must encompass all three dimensions. In an effort to establish such a definition, we offer several criteria to be applied in the design and implementation of academic programs:

Attractive:	It does something that brings people to it.
Beneficial:	It does something that is helpful to the individuals and the community involved in it.
Congruent:	It does what it says it will do.
Distinctive:	It is responsive to the unique characteristics of the institution and its people and thus is unlike most other programs.
Effective:	It does what it does very well and can demonstrate its effectiveness to others.
Functional:	It provides learners with attributes needed to perform successfully in today's society.
Growth producing:	It enhances growth in a number of important directions of learning.

The first five of these criteria of quality focus primarily on the characteristics of the program, while the last two focus primarily on characteristics of the learner who is participating in the program. Following is a more detailed description of each of these criteria.

Attractive. An educational program should be appealing to students, to parents, to the local or sponsoring community, to potential funding sources, and to the people (faculty, administrators, staff) who must conduct the program. An attractive program will be a quantitatively successful program. It will bring students, financial support, and institutional recognition. To be attractive, an educational program must be responsive to the needs and interests of specific populations of current or potential students. If successful, it will also anticipate the emerging needs of potential students and hence will continue to be attractive in the future.

Beneficial. An educational program can be attractive yet not be of highest quality if it ignores the pressing and important problems, needs, and concerns of the community and society in which it exists. An educational program of high quality will be beneficial to students, faculty, and staff (the community of learners) in their growth, development, and learning, and, ultimately, to the community and society beyond the campus.

Congruent. Educational experiences are qualitatively power-ful if they deliver on what is promised by the institution—if what is proposed is true. When high quality is present, stated beliefs and attitude are congruent with behavior. Expressed values are congruent with individual life-styles and institutional decisions. Relationships with people are honest. There is a congruence among intentions, experiences, and outcomes (Argyris and Schön, 1974).

Distinctive. Frequently, educational programs that are at-tractive, beneficial, and congruent at one institution are copied by other institutions without full consideration of the compati-bility and appropriateness of the program for the adapting in-stitution. As a result, when placed in the new setting, the adapted program often loses its attractiveness, its beneficial impact, and especially its congruence. A college or university that seeks to develop a program of highest quality must look to its own unique history, mission, purpose, style, resources, and projected future to find guidance in designing the program.

A high-quality program will not be different merely for the sake of difference. Rather, it will be different from programs at other institutions because it reflects the particular purpose, nature, and people of the institution in which it is offered. This emphasis on the unique character or culture of an organization has become particularly popular at the present time as a result of the success of Thomas Peters and Robert Waterman, Jr.'s *In Search of Excellence* (Peters and Waterman, 1982) and the re-cent increased interest in organizational culture (for example, Schein, 1985).

Effective. Rhetoric can easily push aside performance when the topic of quality is addressed. A new program can readily be devised that, on paper, appears to be attractive, beneficial, congruent, and distinctive. The program will be of highest quality, however, only when intended learning outcomes have been defined clearly and when achievement of these outcomes has been documented and communicated persuasively. A pro-gram cannot be considered to be of highest quality until an in-stitution has taken the risk of specifying and evaluating how it is meeting its intended outcomes. Academic planning should not be just an exercise in design. It should also be an exercise in implementation and evaluation, requiring a concern for the specification, achievement, and evaluation of learning outcomes.

Functional. At the heart of any academic planning effort should be a basic concern for the impact on the individual learner. However elaborate or interesting our interpretations of society, programs, and institutions might be, the ultimate test of effectiveness is how the program meets the needs of and produces desirable change in the current or potential students it intends to serve. An educational program of high quality will provide liberal learning and focused experiences that, through a variety of arrangements, sequences, and conditions, will prepare and assist learners to develop the intellectual, personal, vocational, ethical, and attitudinal attributes that they will need to function in the complex, rapidly changing society of the future (Bergquist, 1976).

Growth Producing. A program of high quality will provide ways to assess each learner's needs and help him or her to grow and develop in mature and satisfying ways. Cognitive, affective, ethical, moral, social, physical, and interpersonal dimensions of development will be taken into account. The learner's developmental needs will be matched by programs and processes that best serve these needs. The more diverse the learner population, the more variations in response there must be to meet the developmental needs of the learners.

Using These Criteria. Keeping in mind these seven criteria of high quality and their application to educational programs and the institutions and the learners involved, we invite your college or university to use our planning model in the review and consideration of current and potential academic programs for high quality development. We do not suggest that traditional quantitative indicators of quality be abandoned; we do suggest, however, that a college or university's curricular review efforts should encourage the leaders of the institution to supplement conventional indicators of quality with indicators that are often more elusive yet in many ways more satisfying.

Indicators of Potential Program Impact

In selecting and developing an academic program of high quality, college and university leaders must examine quality from a number of different perspectives—some quite practical and even political. Several different programs at a college or university may exhibit the seven indicators of high quality discussed above. To be of highest quality, however, a program also should exhibit two aspects of impact: penetration and enablement.

Penetration (Depth of Impact). Patricia Cross (1975) has spoken of the three curricula that exist in every college and university: the curriculum that is described in the institution's bulletin or catalogue (Level One), the curriculum that is being taught by the faculty (Level Two), and the curriculum that is learned by the students (Level Three). Cross notes that the nature and scope of these three curricula are not always the same or even complementary. The institutional curriculum is frequently ignored or contradicted by faculty in their teaching and even more frequently by students in what they learn. Academic planning projects conducted by a college or university often penetrate only to the first of these three curricular levels. As a result of major curriculum change efforts, institutions will alter their calendars or clocks, their use of institutional space or procedures, or even the content or desired outcomes of the curriculum. These changes are reflected in the bulletin and in the official rhetoric of the institution but often not in actual practice (Level Two) or actual outcomes (Level Three). An academic planning initiative should be able to penetrate to Levels Two and Three. An academic program that resists penetration to these levels should be avoided.

A new computer literacy program in a large research university, for instance, was touted as a major breakthrough in undergraduate education. Students would learn how to use the computer not only as a computational tool but also as a tool for word processing and the simulation of complex physical and social systems. In order for this new initiative to penetrate to the second and third levels, academic administrators at this university needed to provide professional development workshops for all faculty regarding the use of computers in the classroom and in their own disciplines (Level Two). Unless the faculty members were themselves comfortable with computers, the students would pick up nothing more than the faculty members' anxieties regarding computers and their use in academic fields. The university also had to negotiate with a major computer company to make desk-top computers available at low cost to students and had to redesign electrical circuits, desks, and lighting in the dormitories to accommodate the new personal computers (Level Three). Computers had to become part of the daily life of students and faculty if the university was to make good on its commitment to computer literacy for all of its students.

Enablement (Breadth of Impact). If an academic program that is selected for highest quality development is to enhance the quality of education throughout the college or university, the program not only should exhibit the seven indicators of quality at all three curricular levels (penetration) but also should increase the probability that other academic programs at the college or university will exhibit these characteristics as well.

An "enabling" program of highest quality will be linked to other programs. It will provide the institution with needed recognition, the faculty, administration, and/or staff with needed resources, and the students with needed skills or experiences to successfully complete other tasks. Even more important, through its successful penetration to all three levels of the curriculum, a successful academic planning initiative will provide encouragement to other program units and will serve as a model for future program development—provided the program is selected in a manner that promotes trust and collaboration among all the campus constituencies.

At a large community college in California, for instance, the faculty recently deliberated about the initiation of new programs in allied health, recreation, liberal arts, and management. While each of these program areas was important to the local community and had strong support on campus, the college could afford to begin only one program at that time. Rather than getting into a struggle over priorities, the faculty and academic administrators of the college decided to reflect on the extent to which each of these programs would enable other programs on campus to be successful and, even more importantly, would enable the other three programs under consideration to begin within the next two years. They discovered that the new management program would bring in needed funds from the business community and would effectively supplement the curricula of the other three new programs. By using the concept of enablement, this college was able to begin the management program without alienating supporters of the three other new program areas.

Looking Ahead

The primary purpose of this book concerns the achievement of highest quality development for educational programs in contemporary colleges and universities. This development is described in terms of a specific planning model first created by staff and consultants to the Council of Independent Colleges for use in assisting sixty small liberal arts colleges in the high quality development of specific academic programs over a four-year period. The faculty, administrators, staff, and students of these colleges further refined this model through its use in the development of a wide variety of academic programs. In Chapter Two, attention is given to the principles that underlie the Academic Planning Model. The chapters in Part Two of this book provide a detailed description of this model, while the lessons learned from the use of this model in the sixty colleges participating in the Quality Undergraduate Education Project (Project QUE) are identified and discussed in the last chapter.

Overview of the Project

Project QUE was designed as a unique, far-reaching project to provide programs and services to a selected number of independent colleges that wished to create a high degree of educational quality within a single academic program (called the ''target academic program'') at their institutions. The concept of having each college select and develop a single target academic program (TAP) was followed for two reasons. First, it would encourage each college to regard the program as having great potential for promoting the growth and development of the individual undergraduate student. Second, each participating college also would be able to concentrate on using and learning a process of academic reform incorporating special knowledge, skills, and methods that could be applied to strengthen other areas of the curriculum after the completion of Project QUE.

A campus team at each college was the basic vehicle for developing that institution's TAP. Over a four-year period, each campus team worked through a series of phases and procedures in the selection, design, testing, and implementation of that program. Another critical component of Project QUE was the involvement of the president of each participating college. Activities were designed to support his or her role in providing strong educational leadership for the college, including the president's participation on the campus team.

Eighty-six institutions participated in the first phase of Project QUE. This phase involved selecting a target academic program and deciding whether to submit a proposal for the development of that program. In the spring of 1980, an external review panel judged the quality of proposals submitted by sixty-eight colleges that wished to continue participation in Project QUE. Of these sixty-eight proposals, forty-five were accepted unconditionally. Twenty-three colleges were asked to revise their proposals, and fifteen did so acceptably. Thus, sixty institutions began the second phase of the project. These were considered the participating colleges in Project QUE. One college discontinued participation during the second phase, seven colleges during the third phase, and two colleges during the fourth phase. Thus, the final roster for the project consisted of fifty colleges.

Achieving Quality
Through Effective Planning

To Plan or Not to Plan

In contemporary colleges and universities, one typically begins with the assumption that planning is a good thing. It would be bad form in most academic settings to question the validity of systematic planning processes. Only the old "dinosaurs" of the institution, who still believe that foreign languages should be required or that a liberal arts education should begin with the classics, are inclined to voice disapproval about this modernistic approach to a college's or university's problems and future. Yet, just as the old dinosaurs might be right about the value of foreign-language requirements and might provide a valuable antidote to overeager dismissal of ancient truths, so should the basic validity of academic planning always be subject to review and discussion.

There are several excellent reasons for questioning the value and even propriety of systematic academic planning. First, effective planning may often involve a great deal more inspiration, creativity, and sheer intuition than most systematic planning processes will allow. Robert Peck (1983, pp. 8–9), formerly vice-president of the Council of Independent Colleges, recently conducted an extensive study of highly successful small-college presidents and found that:

> they would lose control of their institutions if they
> tried to plan and operate the way the experts say
> they should. The theoretical basis for conventional
> planning systems is systematically deductive. It

calls for organizational stability and suggests management structures in which variations systematically are either cancelled out or suppressed. There is no place in such systems for intuition, innovation, or opportunism because the theory presumes no need for them.

What one finds on successful campuses, however, is an entirely different system and an entirely different theory, one in which intuition, innovation, and opportunism are not only present but essential. The reasons are not merely that the organizations are systematically unstable, but the whole environment in which they live and function is ambiguous, uncertain, and unpredictable in principle. And, more important, people do not behave in the highly rational way which management theory presupposes.

In practical terms, what one observes is a whole range of activities, the purpose of which is to anticipate change, identify opportunities, and retain flexibility. These activities are carried out by leaders who are ready to move and willing to take the necessary risks.

Peck's findings should lead us to be cautious about overselling the benefits of systematic planning and to be open to the lessons that these more intuitive planners can teach us. Clearly, we must avoid planning processes that are too confining and that in some manner dampen the human spirit and imagination.

Second, we must avoid the overmanagement that often attends a systematic planning process. Contemporary society may have created a monster that it can no longer control when the tools of modern management—management information systems, management by objectives, and so forth—were introduced. These tools were all created to serve humanistic ends as well as increase organizational productivity, yet they may have lost something of value in promoting efficiency and rationality—namely, a concern for those human traits, capacities, and creations that can not readily be measured or even specified with

precision. We may have created an organizational machine
without a heart or soul—or an organizational machine that effectively "manages" the heart and soul and in this way diminishes an individual's (and the organization's) capacity for independent thought and action (Foucault, 1977; Sennett, 1980;
Briskin, 1984). While the solution to the complex problems that
have been introduced by this form of social critique is certainly
not a return to premanagement days when autocratic rule was
prevalent, we must be cautious in our optimism about systematic
planning as an agent for both increased productivity and human-
ization of the work environment.

What case, then, can be made for systematic planning
in an academic setting? First, academic planning encourages
those involved to make explicit their assumptions about the ways
in which their institution operates, about the probable impact
of various forces that are operating from within and without
their college or university, and about the ways in which an idea
they have about improving their program, department, and so
on relates to broader institutional missions, constraints, and
resources. Not only does systematic planning encourage this
revealing of hidden plans and assumptions; it also encourages
an orderliness in this revelation, such that one person's ideas,
assumptions, and perceptions can be related to another person's.
In this sense, systematic academic planning is nothing more than
an aid to discussion. It is certainly not a panacea. When effectively conducted, however, a systematic planning process will
reduce the number and intensity of problems confronted by a
collegiate institution in its future.

Another excellent case that can be made for systematic
academic planning centers on the often demobilizing and demoralizing effect of unpredictable futures. Increasingly, we seem
as educators (and even more generally as citizens) to be confronted with complex and rapidly changing conditions that do
not allow us to make successful predictions about either our individual or our collective futures. How can one plan anything,
when federal funding is so unpredictable? Why should I have
to make a painful decision concerning program priorities, when
the students' interests may take us in a different direction two

years from now, anyway? How can you expect my department to be accountable for its goals in a two-year plan, when economic and political conditions that directly affect my program will probably change significantly during this period of time? Typically, a sense of powerlessness accompanies this recognition of unpredictability. While the large size of most organizations is usually identified as the primary source of this sense of powerlessness, the unpredictability factor may be just as important.

Systematic academic planning can help reduce this often pervasive sense of powerlessness by encouraging members of an organization to draw up several alternative responses to a variety of possible future conditions. This mode of systematic planning—called strategic planning—empowers people and diminishes their fear of unpredictable futures. As a result, action will occur, based on careful reflection. The caution of unpredictability is balanced by the boldness of planning for direct response to alternative futures.

Shorter-term modes of planning—usually called tactical planning—provide for various contingencies of a more immediate nature. According to Martorana and Kuhns (1975, pp. 162–63), "a strategy is an overall plan of action for achieving a goal," whereas "tactics are the specific actions taken to implement chosen strategies. Both strategies and tactics imply movement toward the achievement of predetermined goals. Strategies are the more encompassing plans for action; within the limits set by the goals strategies provide the broad parameters for action. Tactics are ways of carrying out strategies. Tactics are trial and error phenomena; they are expendable."

Variability in day-to-day conditions that an organization faces is confronted through the development of a specific tactical plan that takes this variability into account. The tactical plan must be able to accommodate those short-term shifts that can be anticipated in any complex, contemporary environment. As Peck (1983) noted in his study of the entrepreneurial college presidency, a boldness and creativity that can take advantage of short-term opportunities must accompany any planning effort. Otherwise, the planning effort will hamper rather than help a college or university in its anticipation of a changing world.

These arguments in favor of systematic planning require that this process be conceived in a new way. The arguments that can be made against systematic planning further encourage us to define the process in a new way. The Academic Planning Model that is proposed in this chapter is designed to yield the desirable results and avoid the undesirable pitfalls that are described above.

Linear Versus Cyclical Planning

Most models of systematic planning are linear in nature. They spell out specific steps that must be taken in a certain sequential order. Typically, a planning model will begin with some specification of goals or mission for the organization, department, and so on. It will then move to the collection of information about the gaps that exist in the organization with reference to these goals; that is, where the organization is now falling short in accomplishing these goals or this mission. In a consumer-oriented enterprise such as a college or university, this second step usually takes the form of assessing the current needs of the consumer/client population (in this case, students or potential employers).

Planning then moves to the identification of alternative strategies that would enable the organization to meet these identified needs and the selection of a specific strategy from among those identified. Implementation and monitoring of the selected strategy then follow, often with an intermediate step concerned with determining the best way in which to introduce this strategy into the organization, usually borrowing from the ''planned change'' and/or ''dissemination of innovation'' literature (Lindquist, 1978b; Rogers, 1983). A final step usually is concerned with the formal evaluation of the new program after a certain period of time, followed by decision-making concerning its continuation, as well as modification, expansion, or reduction in its scope or nature.

One example of a linear planning model is offered by Zaltman, Florio, and Sikorski (1977, p. 127). This thorough ten-step model illustrates the best of those linear models that are particularly sensitive to the dynamics of planned change:

1. Identify the organizational mission by stating the goals and objectives explicitly.
2. Identify problems.
3. Assess needs.
4. Identify resources and constraints.
5. Structure alternative courses of action in light of available resources and existing or forthcoming constraints and barriers, both within the system and in the environment.
6. Build alternative strategies for problem solving.
7. Build alternative strategies for resource use.
8. Build alternative strategies for testing alternatives.
9. Build alternative strategies for making decisions.
10. Build alternative strategies for evaluating changes or innovations in the light of goals and objectives.

This model is representative of those now available and widely used. It can be quite valuable in identifying the essential features of any effective planning process. It falls short, however, in several respects. First, it does not accurately describe the way in which effective planning often takes place under normal conditions. As Peck (1983) noted, a college president may pick up planning at any point in the process. An academic dean may initiate a new interdisciplinary program without first doing a needs assessment because she believes that this program will actually generate a need that is not now present. A director of institutional research may argue that we must first collect information about the existing resources of the university (funds, faculty, expertise, facilities, and so on) before identifying the future direction (goals) of the university. A faculty member may introduce a new course on a trial basis at his college because he wants to demonstrate that it can be done, even with limited resources.

    Second, this planning model tends to hamper the creativity and spontaneity that are abundant in a collegiate institution. During a planning meeting, some faculty, staff, and administrators will want to present their own pet ideas before dealing with issues of goals, resources, and change strategies. If not allowed to do so, these participants will often feel cut off and devalued and will artfully try to steer the group's decisions about goals, resources, and change strategies in directions that are compatible with their predetermined program ideas. Ironically, a planning team member will often be more willing to abandon his or her own ideas when given an early chance to express them. Sometimes, a planning process must be employed that enables participants to interject their primary concerns at various points in the process without disrupting it. A linear planning model typically requires a much stricter adherence to a specific focus on a specific topic at any one moment in the planning process.

A linear model also typically fails to recognize the close relationship among various steps in a planning process. Chicken-and-egg dilemmas show up throughout an actual, working planning process: "How can we define realistic goals until we identify our existing resources?" "How do we know what resources to look for in this college until we know what the goals will be for this program?" "How can we identify the needs of our students until we know which population of students we wish to serve?" "How do we know which population to serve until we know what our current capacities are to meet the needs of this population?" "How do we know what the needs of this population are?" A linear planning process forces us to answer one of these questions first, thus beginning the process on a weak note, with inadequate information. Effective planning requires a recursive, cyclical process, whereby each question is reintroduced at various points and answers to the questions become progressively more refined and pertinent with the further refinement of other, related planning questions.

Effective planning requires a cyclical process that enables the concerns of participants to be introduced at a variety of points, that encourages creativity and spontaneity, and that provides repeated opportunities for central planning questions to be answered in an increasingly refined and interrelated manner. The key to such a planning process appears to be the recognition that people involved in planning move repeatedly through three different conceptual domains—information, values, and ideas—and that tendencies toward reflection and action in a planning process must continually be balanced against one another. In the following two sections of this chapter, we more fully describe these two principles and relate each to the notion of cyclical planning.

The Problem-Solving Process:
Situation, Target, and Proposal

Each of us deals with problems on a daily basis in any academic setting. Try as we might, we simply cannot avoid them. When we do confront a problem, however, we generally attempt to come up with an immediate solution. Sometimes we succeed. Sometimes, however, what appears to be a good solution soon proves either inadequate or unacceptable. Sometimes we may find that in the long run our "solution" has just created other, still more complex problems.

The linear planning model that was identified in the previous section rightfully suggests that precipitous generation of solutions is inappropriate. Solutions must be geared to the goals of the organization. The assumption is made that problems are often not fully understood or resolved because they have not been stated in terms of goals. Without these guidelines, advocates of these planning models note, we have neither a direction for solution nor a basis for evaluating our actions.

While the specification of goals and objectives is essential for effective problem solving, we must also have a clear picture of the current state in which the problem occurs. Any goal or objective that we might establish runs the risk of being unrealistic or of eventually generating further problems. It is difficult, however, to establish a realistic goal or objective without first understanding the current situation in which the problem resides. Objectives identified without adequate knowledge of existing conditions may look good on paper but become useless or even destructive when achieved. Once we have determined the key characteristics of both current and desired conditions, we can move toward a solution—taking action to change the current conditions into the desired alternative. What we know about a problem can thus be divided into the following interrelated dimensions (Phillips and Bergquist, 1986):

> *The situation:* information about the essential features of
>   the current state.
> *The target:* the desired state—what we want to accomplish
>   and/or to avoid.

> *The proposal:* specific actions to be taken aimed at chang-
> ing the current state into the desired state.

Following are some common expressions and terms that are
associated with these three dimensions:

> *The situation:* starting point, facts, opinions, explanations
> about current state, predictions about change, environ-
> ment as perceived by planners.
> *The target:* terminating point, goals, aims, ends, purposes,
> objectives, desires outcomes.
> *The proposal:* path from situation to target, means, plans,
> strategies, implementation procedures, possible actions.

The Domains of Information, Values, and Ideas. Situation,
target, and proposal not only define the three elements of effective problem-solving and planning; they also define the three
domains in which planning takes place: information, values,
and ideas.

The domain of information is entered whenever we attempt to find out more about the current situation. In soliciting
information, academic planners act as researchers: they ask questions that can be answered by a systematic collection of information. For example, if a college wants to know which of four
academic programs is potentially most attractive to a particular
group of prospective students, then a sample of these students
might be asked to indicate under what conditions they would
be likely to enroll in each of the programs. If the information
obtained is valid—that is, if the students have been honest, if
the right questions were asked, and if the sample used is representative of the entire pool of potential students—then the college should be able to state with some confidence which of the
academic programs is most attractive to this population of potential students.

In understanding the current situation, however, academic
planners must not only seek information that is valid. They must
also seek information that is useful. It must relate to the target
the planners wish to reach. Thus, if the target concerns increased

financial viability for the college, then a market survey will be of little use, even if the information obtained is valid, unless the costs associated with each of the four academic programs also can be determined, along with the acceptable tuition levels for this population of students. It is surprising to see how often information is collected that relates only marginally to the problem faced by an academic organization.

Many problems can be solved through the systematic collection of valid and useful information. This lies at the heart of rational, linear problem-solving and planning processes, an approach that is best represented by the models of Charles Kepner and Benjamin Tregoe (1965) and Lorne Plunkett and Guy Hale (1982). Other problems, unfortunately, cannot be solved merely by collecting information about the current situation. Many problems in higher education—particularly those involving people rather than machines—center, at least in part, on conflicting goals, objectives, or desired outcomes. Attention must shift from the domain of information to that of values. This domain is likely to be particularly dominant in the academic world, where conflict in values is so commonly found.

The domain of values is entered whenever we attempt to understand and clarify targets. While research prevails in the area of information, clarification prevails in the area of values. Unlike traditional approaches to values, which tend to emphasize enforcement or modeling, values clarification focuses on the process of valuing and the way values come into being. As we become clearer about our values, we will begin to produce solutions that are more and more consistent with them.

As Carl Rogers (1964) points out in his discussion of values, the valuing process becomes richer and more profound as each of us moves toward greater maturity. In the mature person, the valuing process is characterized by choosing, prizing, and acting. A value is freely chosen; it is not imposing (an imposed requirement is part of the situation dimension). A value is prized and affirmed; a value is repeatedly acted on. Few of us, however, are wholly mature or are mature all the time. Sometimes, decisions are made and actions are taken that, on later reflection, appear inconsistent with personal or institutional values. A thorough exploration of the domain of values will help ensure that the goals and objectives we are attempting to meet will be more consistently and directly related to our most important values.

The domain of ideas is entered whenever an attempt is made to generate a proposal intended to move from the current to the desired state. Ideas are sometimes fragile, often misunderstood, and easily lost. While information exists everywhere, we often ignore or misinterpret it. But we can usually go back and retrieve it. Similarly, even though values may be ignored or distorted, they resist extinction, and sometimes we are frustrated by their resistance to change. Ideas, on the other hand, are easy to lose and hard to recover. Settings must be created in which ideas can readily be generated and retained. Two processes are essential. The first, divergence, exists in the realm of creative problem solving. Divergence requires minimal censorship of ideas, minimal restriction of self-expression and risk taking, and minimal adherence to prescribed rules or procedures for the generation of new ideas. The second process is convergence. People must be given the opportunity to build on each other's ideas, to identify similarities in their ideas, and to agree upon a desired course of action. Convergence requires planners to observe specific rules and procedures, to listen, and to be constructively critical of other ideas. The domain of ideas often requires planners to display a subtle and skillful interplay between convergence and divergence.

Interaction Among Situation, Target, and Proposal. Effective problem solving and planning will at times move systematically and in a linear fashion from target (values clarification) to situation (information collection) to proposal (idea generation), or from situation to target to proposal. Because these three dimensions are not independent of each other, however, problem solving and planning are best thought of not as a movement from one dimension to another but rather as an interaction among all three. With regard to the relationship between situation and target, dissatisfaction with the current situation implies a particular target as a standard of comparison. Program planning is impelled sometimes by lofty goals rather than by an inadequacy in the current conditions of a college or university. Conversely, any suggested goal implies by comparison what is unsatisfactory about the current situation.

With regard to the relationship between target and proposal, a target defines the results desired from any proposal. As noted in most planning models, one cannot adequately review or evaluate various proposals without defining first the end to be reached by them. On the other hand, any proposal embodies assumptions about the nature of the desired target—a planning group can often clarify their goals by generating and discussing several different proposals.

Proposals and situational assessments frequently interact with one another in an effective planning process. A proposal embodies assumptions about the causes of an unsatisfactory situation and implies resources and requirements for change, as well as the probable sources of resistance to the change. Conversely, information about the current situation places limits on the effectiveness and feasibility of specific proposals that have been generated.

Because these three dimensions are so clearly interrelated, it is helpful to think of them as a single interacting unit rather than as three separate factors related to each other in a straight-line sequence. Furthermore, it is often effective to work on all three dimensions at once rather than one at a time. Those who plan academic programs should be free to discuss the values inherent in the plans that are formulated, to collect and analyze information associated with these plans, and to generate ideas about how the college or university can become better (values), given its current resources, needs, and precedence (information). The form in which the values, information, and ideas will be organized need not dictate the form of the inquiry itself.

In the process of program planning, it is possible to translate statements about one dimension into statements about other dimensions, since each dimension is related to the other two. When information is generated about the situation, target values can be elicited by such questions as: "If you could change the present situation, what would you want to accomplish?" "What is missing in the present situation that you want?" "What would be your goal in improving this situation?'' Proposal ideas can be generated from a situational statement by such questions as: ''What might be done to improve that?'' ''What kind of action does that seem to require?'' ''What plan would use that resource?'' When a target is identified, situational information can be elicited by such questions as: ''In what ways does the present situation fall short of that goal?'' ''Why does the present situation fall short of that goal?'' ''What forces for improvement are there for reaching that goal?'' ''What obstacles stand in the way of reaching that goal?'' Proposals can be elicited from a target statement by asking: ''What might be a possible way to accomplish that?'' ''What steps might lead toward that goal?'' In a similar manner, when a proposal presents itself, situational information can be elicited by asking: ''What might that improve in the present situation?'' ''What part of the plan do you see that dealing with?'' ''What resources are there for doing that?'' Finally, target values can be elicited from the proposal by asking: ''To accomplish what?'' ''In order to do what?'' ''What goals or objectives does that proposal aim at?''

Program planning often seems to wander aimlessly from topic to topic without ever actually coming to grips with a specific plan. By categorizing statements according to situation, target, or proposal, and by using statements in one dimension to bring forth statements in other dimensions, one can help a planning group move systematically toward formulation of a proposal, without locking itself into a linear process.

Reflection and Action

An effective planning model not only blends information, values, and ideas but also balances phases of reflection and action. Frequently, an academic planning committee will either spend too much time in reflection and never move beyond untested ideas or move precipitously toward action with insufficient attention to either information or values. Effective planning requires a balancing of the two. In providing this balance, a committee must look, on the one hand, toward the "activist." He or she is to be found on any planning committee—and at times typifies an entire committee. This person or group dwells in a world of ideas and action. Things are to be done immediately. For the activist, cautious deliberations are frustrating and demoralizing: "Let's get on with it!" The activist tends to define the world in terms of leadership and risk taking. He or she often suspects that the real problem of those who urge more deliberation is an unwillingness to take risks. The activist believes that action must be taken even though not all the information is in and even though the proposed solution is not perfect.

On the other hand, a planning committee must also look for sources of reflection. These people tend to be oriented toward either "realism" or "idealism." Whereas the "activist" wants to dwell in the domain of ideas, the "realist" wants to remain in the domain of information and the "idealist" in the domain of values. The activist views the idealist as hopelessly romantic—a person who would rather build castles in the air than construct a durable bungalow on earth. Similarly, the realist is perceived by the activist as being an immobile, often obsessive man or woman of "facts." The realist never lifts up his or her head long enough or far enough to see what is actually happening in the world.

Planning groups are often pulled not only between reflection and action but also between realism and idealism. The realistic group member or planning group is careful and cautious, because of concern that problems may be "solved" through wishful thinking (the failure of idealism) or without anticipating the consequences (the failure of activism). Like the realist, the idealist is cautious and reflective—but not for a lack of adequate information. The idealist or idealistically oriented planning team is concerned about a confusion between means and ends—about losing the war while seeming to win individual battles through expedience. The idealist confronts the realist with his or her lack of courage: if bold vision is lacking, then when will risks be taken and progress made? On the other hand, within minutes of formulating a new academic program, the idealist is imagining how things could be improved. He or she challenges the mundane reasoning of the realist and notes that new perspectives are needed on old problems if the activist is to be successful in generating proposals to solve these problems.

Effective planning—whether done individually or in a group—requires a balance between or even an integration of these different perspectives. "Pragmatism" requires that realism, idealism, and activism be combined. Effective planning will shift among the domains of information, values, and ideas. When confronted with a new, unpredictable situation, a pragmatic academic planner will tend to become realistic by attempting to assimilate this new reality. When confronted with an old, unchanging environment, the pragmatic planner will tend to become a daydreamer, creating images of how this environment might be quite different from and better than it now is. When confronted with the press of time and the press of events, the pragmatist will tend to mobilize his or her activism, creating proposals to meet these challenges.

All three of the extreme planning preferences tend in some settings to be ineffective and to create more problems than they solve. Reflection must be balanced against action. Furthermore, the period of reflection must provide opportunities for both the collection of new information and the clarification of existing values. An effective balancing and integration of reflection and action requires that action produce and be based on information, that action inform and clarify values, and that reflection lead to decision and action.

Any planning group needs one or more pragmatists to provide some balance and integration. However, the pragmatist may enter one of the three domains at the wrong time and in this way produce many of the destructive outcomes that are associated with one of the three extreme types described above. In some instances, a group can be very effective in academic planning if it contains members representing each of the three extreme types, rather than a preponderance of pragmatists. Realists, idealists, and activists can build on each other's efforts—if they each acknowledge the worth of the other two perspectives—and can ensure that each aspect of the academic planning process is being given adequate attention.

The Academic Planning Model

The Academic Planning Model proposed here blends the collection of information with the identification and clarification of values and the generation of imaginative yet realistic academic program proposals. This model also moves a planning group through cycles of reflection and action. Although this cyclical model differs in its actual implementation from program to program and from college to college, it typically incorporates five phases that are flexibly interwoven with each institution's own methods of operation.

Phase One: Selecting a Target Academic Program. The first phase of the Academic Planning Model helps a college, university, or unit of an institution develop consensus around the need for change in a particular program area. This phase blends the generation of information with the clarification of values, while encouraging a planning group to spend some time reflecting before moving to action. Depending on the type of institution and the magnitude of change under consideration, this initiative typically begins with study and commitment on the part of the president, the chief academic officer, and key faculty and administrators and then moves to discussion within the large college or university community or the affected segment of that community. Because consensus about the need for change and the area in which it will occur is crucial to the project's success, the first phase of the Academic Planning Model is extremely important. Many academic change efforts ultimately fail because insufficient attention is given to this initial phase of planning.

Phase Two: Identifying the Outcomes for a Target Academic Program. The second phase of the Academic Planning Model emphasizes both reflection and action, while focusing on both the collection of information and the initial consideration of alternative plans. During this phase, a campus team or committee is formed to identify the desired outcomes for a program that incorporates existing knowledge about student development.

Phase Three: Designing a Target Academic Program. During this phase, emphasis is placed on the initial design of an ideal program that is responsive to the outcomes that have been identified during the second phase. Following this, more data about available and needed resources are collected with specific reference to the ideally designed program. A more realistic design is then developed, based on these data. Throughout the design process, the planning group is encouraged to study alternative program designs that may be available from other colleges and universities. Communication with other campuses can be helpful, since limited resources require expedient use of time and money. However, colleges and universities are also encouraged to move beyond the perspectives and practices of sister institutions and to form their own approaches and solutions. The use of workshops and carefully selected external consultations is often quite important during this phase.

Phase Four: Pilot-Testing, Assessing, and Refining a Target Academic Program. Phase Four of the Academic Planning Model helps a college or university to pilot test a new program before fully implementing it. Most academic planners are skilled in designing promising new programs and even successful in guiding them through ultimate adoption by the faculty. Unfortunately, these very planners are often the most surprised and disappointed when new programs fail to achieve the great things originally expected of them. The key to successful program implementation is found in taking time for pilot testing.

Pilot testing provides a supportive environment for action in which information can be collected and proposals can be generated. It also provides an environment in which those planning the program can determine whether the goals and objectives of the program are actually those most desired—at least as experienced in the pilot test. In this setting, faculty and academic administrators function as learners as well as teachers. Professional performance is analyzed and criticized constructively and in detail. Pilot testing also encourages learning about outcomes assessment and testing program evaluation methods.

Phase Five: Implementing an Academic Program. The final phase of the Academic Planning Model helps a college or university to implement, evaluate, and modify a new program and to disseminate information about knowledge gained to other colleges and universities. This phase centers in action yet still encourages reflection on knowledge gained from the planning process. The learning gained from this reflection can then be applied to future improvements of this program or of other programs being conducted by the college or university or by other collegiate institutions.

Timing the Planning Process. The five phases of the Academic Planning Model are usually implemented over a three- to four-year period; however, the timing of the phases can readily be adapted to meet the specific needs of each college or university. Some collegiate institutions or academic departments, for instance, may require five or six years, while others complete the process in less than two years. One college with which the authors have worked spent three years in simply cultivating a discussion about the nature of liberal education, before embarking on an additional three years of planning and design of a new general education curriculum. Given that this college has built its reputation on the general education program it offers and went through a very destructive revision of the general education curriculum in the recent past, this slow, cautious process was appropriate. A major state university with which one of the authors has worked, on the other hand, moved into a major new field of technology within one year. This rapid process was possible because of this institution's clear identification with technological education and was necessitated by the rapid rise of this field of technology in the region.

What are the factors that seem to influence the appropriate length of a planning process? The two instances just cited point to the importance of three factors: (1) level of significance of the program area to the overall mission of the institution (or unit of the institution), (2) compatibility of the program area with the existing mission and image of the institution, and (3) demand for rapid implementation of the program from within or outside the institution. From Project QUE, the authors further concluded that an intensive planning effort could be completed in less than one year, if the change effort is not of great magnitude (for example, shift in two units of a sixteen-unit survey of Western civilization course).

Regardless of the time that is required, the Academic Planning Model provides valuable guidelines regarding the timely and effective movement among the domains of information, values, and ideas while planning for an academic program of high quality.

%%%%% 3 %%%%%

Targeting a Program for
Development or Improvement

Setting the Context

College and university leaders face a significant task in identifying a program for high quality development, whether that development be directed toward strengthening an existing program or creating a new program. If this phase of the planning process is to be successful, certain assumptions must be made about how the eight steps in this phase are to be negotiated. These assumptions, in turn, translate into particular approaches or strategies for program planning.

There are four different assumptions and related approaches that might be taken in completing Phase One tasks: rational, political, informal, and participative (Sashkin, Morris, and Horst, 1973; Lindquist, 1978b; Huse, 1975; Argyris, 1970; Lippitt, Watson, and Westley, 1958; Schein, 1969). Each of these is appropriate for some colleges and universities and inappropriate for others. However, the participative approach is particularly appropriate in completing the often controversial tasks of establishing priorities, formulating selection criteria, and ultimately choosing one program for highest quality development. Following are some of our thoughts, as well as some of the Project QUE college experiences, regarding these four assumptions and their relative strengths and weaknesses in helping guide the leaders of a college or university through Phase One of the planning model.

The Rational Approach. The assumption behind this approach to program selection is that members of the campus community will accept and support the program that can be most rationally defended as the best program to be developed by the college or university. Issues of jealousy, turf, and power are ignored or considered unfortunate blemishes in the rational planning process.

Institutions of higher education are, of course, devoted to the promotion of rationality. Since people change on the basis of reason (the rational approach assumes), the best method of program selection is to present an extensively documented and researched proposal to the campus community. A planning team should be selected on the basis of research skills and expertise. Using this approach, the planning team would invest considerable energy in both institutional and program research. The limitations of such a strategy are often disillusioning. A planning team following the rational approach usually works in isolation from the larger community. The problems, solutions, and compromises with which the planning team has struggled would be neither experienced nor perhaps understood by the rest of the institution. Furthermore, even though we are rational beings, we are also at times emotional and irrational. No matter how fully documented, a proposal that threatens vested interests, departmental autonomy, or disciplinary territory will not be received rationally. Although reasons and careful documentation are absolutely necessary, particularly in higher education, they are not sufficient. Other approaches must be sought to supplement the rational approach.

The Political Approach. If reason will not work, perhaps a political strategy will, since faculty and institutional governance exist to allow us to work together as colleagues in the mutual exchange of ideas. Using the political approach, a planning team composed of elected campus leaders and chairpersons of key committees and/or academic departments would turn to the appropriate standing committee for selection of the academic program that is to receive extensive attention. The selected program would be debated and voted on by that group, and the planning team would then move its program through the college or university governance structure. After some negotiation and perhaps revision, the final program would be voted on by the appropriate campus group(s).

Some of the Project QUE schools employed a political approach in selecting and designing their target academic programs. Typically, these were colleges that attempted to use Project QUE to review and reform the general education program of the institution. One would expect in such cases that a political approach would be appropriate, though often troublesome.

At Rust College (Mississippi), for instance, a College-Wide Inter-Disciplinary Committee on Competency-Based Instruction was established in 1979. Meeting regularly each week throughout the academic year, this committee was chaired by the academic dean and involved the active participation of student representatives from each division, division chairpersons, and faculty representatives. Rust College was quite successful in establishing this committee and charging it with primary responsibility for researching and designing a new competency-based program. The success of this committee might in part be due to the use of not only political but also rational approaches to program selection and planning; it made extensive use of a distinguished and internationally recognized authority on competency-based education. Faculty and academic administrators at another liberal arts college were apparently much less successful than the faculty and administrators at Rust College, however, in using the political approach to reforming their collegewide program. Case Study One provides a brief description of the problems encountered at this college.

CASE STUDY ONE
"Anonymous College"

Target Academic Program: General Education
Primary Source: Anonymous

At this small liberal arts college, the faculty focused on general education for high quality development, employing a political approach. Since this program necessarily involved all elements of the academic community at the college, the faculty as a total group first reviewed and adopted a conceptual scheme for a new general education curriculum in January 1982. Interdisciplinary design teams were then appointed in February to flesh out the major areas of the overall scheme. A new general education committee was proposed as a standing committee of the faculty that would preside over the core curriculum. This proposal failed to receive the necessary two-thirds majority approval for inclusion in the faculty constitution. The project director reported that as of May 1982, there was "significant progress in one or two design teams" but only "'soft support' for the overall project."

During the following fall, the design teams were encouraged to continue. Timetables were presented such that "trial runs" could be conducted of new introductory courses in each of several breadth areas during the fall of 1983. Faculty approval for these new courses, however, was required by December 1982. In November, the Curriculum Review Committee received design proposals from several of the design teams and prepared a set of course proposals for the Academic Policy and Procedures Committee of the college. In December, this committee decided to take "no action" on any of the proposals from the Curriculum Review Committee and began its own investigations of the status of the present curriculum study. As a result, the Curriculum Review Committee, which had been an ad hoc committee for Project QUE, was "dead in the water."

The project director speculated that if the Policies and Procedures Committee did take a leading role, it might move curricular study into the faculty's mainstream at the college. In this case, according to the director, "there is a strong possibility that the overall scheme given provisional approval last January [1982] will perish from being 'tabled.'"

This case suggests some of the difficulties encountered by colleges and universities that embark on the political road to curriculum development. Various constituencies and factions of the institution will compete not only for acceptance of different program ideas but also for levels of influence in the whole design process. Curricular plans that have been carefully formulated and documented often become "political footballs" and are relegated prematurely to the scrap heap of good ideas. While political strategies are frequently necessary for gaining formal acceptance of a curricular plan, a design team should usually build in broad-based participation from the start of the Phase One selection process, so that a powerful momentum is built that can be sustained against even the most skillful political counteraction.

At least three limitations to the political approach are apparent. First, it may take too long. Even if it were feasible for the planning team to work through the various levels of institutional governance, in most institutions the process would likely not be completed within an acceptable period of time. Second, the amount of energy available for Phase One planning is finite. Time that is spent in establishing an appropriate political approach may not be effort spent in generating the best possible proposal or in implementing the most successful program. Successful passage does not necessarily mean a successful academic program. Many academic programs fail because those faculty members who move the proposal through the elaborate labyrinth of a collegiate governance system are too exhausted or discouraged at the end of this process to initiate the approved program. Third, faculty and college governance systems may produce solutions and plans that are politically acceptable but not always educationally sound.

Nevertheless, it is acknowledged that in many institutions (especially large, complex university systems), the use of the normal governance or planning procedures is the only appropriate program selection process. In most instances, however, even when formal faculty approval is required, academic planning can benefit from a combination of the four approaches described herein.

The Informal Approach. Formal collegiate decision making may be rational and political, advocates of this third approach argue, but real decision making is done informally, socially, and on the basis of personal influence. A planning team holding this assumption would be composed primarily of institutional opinion leaders who, once having selected a program for highest quality development among themselves, would devote their time to informal social contact with their colleagues in an effort to promote the informally selected program. Although the formal process of acceptance might appear rational and/or political, the outcome would have been assured by informal social interaction.

Two problems are likely to be encountered in an exclusive reliance on the informal approach. First, this approach is individually centered. Its strength is also its weakness. In focusing on individual attitudes, the informal approach ignores institutional and organizational attitudes. Social interactions and

networks may simply not be extensive enough or powerful
enough to bring about the kind of institutional commitment that
is demanded by a major academic planning effort.

Second, as with the rational approach, the informal approach largely envisions a passive role for the broader campus
community. The opinion leaders who would make up the majority of the members of a planning team following this approach
would essentially be selling the selected academic program to
their relatively passive colleagues. Even though this might produce apparent agreement, the implementation and active support of the program by those same passive individuals in the
ensuing phases would not be assured. In spite of the power of
informal social interaction, more seems to be required.

The Participative Approach. Common to all three of the approaches to program selection discussed so far is the relative
inactivity of the larger campus community in the decision-
making process. While in various ways the members of the planning team may have invested considerable time and effort in
the project, their colleagues have largely gone about their business undisturbed and perhaps even unaware of the planning project. The most that is required of them is approval of the academic program finally selected, whether that approval is motivated by political alliance, social interaction, or the persuasive-
ness of logical arguments. If no further institutional action were
required, any of these three strategies—or any combination of
them—would seem appropriate. The program selected in Phase
One, however, may need to be designed, tested, and implemented during Phases Three, Four, and Five not by the few
members of the planning team but by a significant number of
their colleagues. If the target academic program that is selected
in Phase One meets the criteria of quality defined in Chapter
One, then ''enablement'' must be kept in mind. Enablement,
in turn, requires that most if not all of the campus community
be knowledgeable about and supportive of the project. Such
broad-based understanding and commitment, advocates of the
participative approach suggest, can be developed only by the
extensive involvement of many different segments of the campus community during Phase One.

A planning team using the participative approach would attempt to design a Phase One planning process that allows for frequent input by the campus community, frequent feedback to the community about the progress of the team, and even occasional involvement of various segments of the community in the decision-making activities. Although much of the actual work of information collection and analysis would be conducted by the planning team, every effort would be made to involve the larger community. In spite of the apparently cumbersome nature of this process, broadbased participation would be sought consistently in the belief that such participation not only helps the institution make the best possible decision but also helps ensure the successful implementation of the academic program in the following phases. Institutional support would be achieved and the chances of producing a high-quality program enhanced.

A Combination of Approaches. No single approach to the selection of an academic program seems adequate in itself. Even the participative approach is likely to fail if divorced from rational and logical presentation of evidence, appropriate use of governance structures and processes, and timely contact with campus opinion leaders. Clearly, the best approach is one that combines all four strategies. The membership of the planning team might deliberately reflect that combination. A team composed of politically skilled opinion leaders, backed by research and writing expertise and group-process skills, would be hard to beat in planning and carrying out the eight steps of Phase One.

Step One: Selecting a
Coordinator and a Planning Committee

- *Responsibilities*
  The coordinator and planning committee are selected by the major academic administrator of the college or university in consultation with other campus leaders or through the selection process normally used by the institution.
- *Tasks to Be Accomplished*
  1. Select the planning coordinator.
  2. Establish criteria for selection of planning committee members.

3.   Select planning committee members.
4.   Inform committee members and arrange for any reassignment of responsibilities, if necessary.

The first step in the academic planning model is the selection of a coordinator and a planning committee. The coordinator should be released from current responsibilities for one-quarter time or more, depending on the scope of the program envisioned. The coordinator is selected specifically for Phase One but, in many instances, functions in this capacity during Phases Two, Three, Four, and Five as well.

The role of the coordinator in Phase One is to provide leadership for and facilitation of the program selection procedure. During this phase, most coordinators in the QUE project were faculty members who were released from teaching one course each semester. This time allocation was found to be sufficient for most QUE colleges during Phase One. In a few cases, an assistant or associate dean had some of his or her regular duties assigned elsewhere to accommodate the coordinator's role. In a few other cases, the academic dean served as coordinator. Usually the institution cited the dean's interest and leadership ability as the important reason for his or her serving in this capacity; although the real reason was sometimes the college's belief that it could not afford the time of anyone else. In many instances, a logical need developed to change coordinators after a program was selected for Project QUE. Special and different expertise was needed to provide leadership during the program design and development phases (Two, Three, Four, and Five). In other instances, it was believed that an able and respected faculty or staff members could provide the necessary facilitation skills, regardless of the person's disciplinary background or the nature of the selected program.

The planning committee at each QUE college was composed of the president and dean of the college and three to five other individuals (usually faculty members, staff members, and/or students). The planning committee typically assumed primary responsibility in Phase One for (1) planning and implementing all community meetings, (2) coordinating the identification, collection, and analysis of information about the college, (3) identifying alternative academic programs, (4) selecting one academic program for development, and (5) preparing a summary report for Phase Two. Given the extent of these responsibilities, QUE project staff in Washington, D.C., urged that the task not be assigned to an already overworked standing committee of the college, such as the curriculum or academic affairs committee. These staff concerns were justified, for several projects never received the attention that they should have on campus because of conflicting priorities for the standing committee.

Although each college was to select planning committee members in a manner that reflected its own unique governance process and particular staff resources, several criteria for the selection of planning committee members seemed to be of common value:

1. *Credibility:* formal credentials, past performance, reputation, past leadership, objectivity, trustworthiness, orientation to institutional good.
2. *Interest:* past history of involvement in similar efforts, openness to new perspectives and program ideas.
3. *Available time:* lack of overcommitment at the present time, past record of responsible time management.
4. *Expertise:* experience in curriculum and program development, knowledge about current trends in higher education, previous task force experience, strong interpersonal skills, experience in proposal and grant writing.

For many Project QUE colleges, the most important of these criteria seemed to be available time. With available time, Project QUE task force members were less likely to "burn out." They tended to remain on the task force throughout the four years of its existence and the completion of the Academic Planning Model. This continuity of membership proved to be an important ingredient in determining project success for many QUE colleges. At Spelman College (Georgia), for instance, "one of the strengths of the QUE Team members [was] the continuity [of membership]: about half of the QUE Team members [were] with the project for at least two years" (Drake, 1982).

Those Project QUE colleges whose teams were composed of the coordinator, faculty members, students, the dean, and the president often achieved considerable success in their program selection and planning endeavors. Nevertheless, while carefully conceived roles and responsibilities proved useful to many of the Project QUE colleges when they were beginning the Academic Planning Model, one must appreciate the complexities and unanticipated events that often influence committee membership and require adjustments and accommodations. A case study from Trinity College (Vermont) illustrates this need for adaptability (see Case Study Two).

CASE STUDY TWO
Trinity College
Burlington, Vermont

Target Academic Program: Freshman Advisement Seminar
Primary Source: Rodd (1983)

At Trinity College, a small personalized advising seminar was developed to serve the college's traditional-aged (eighteen- to twenty-two-year-old) entering freshmen (all of whom are women). According to the project coordinator at Trinity College, "the campus team was at the heart of the seminar program's development" (p. 1). After the first year, membership remained quite stable. Team participation was fullest in the early, conceptual stages of the project. As the target academic program became clearly defined, some nonfaculty members of the team who saw the chosen academic program as outside their area of interest (because it was basically curricular and involved only traditional-aged students) gradually lessened their commitment. However, a core of highly committed faculty members remained, two of whom have become seminar instructors.

Two students were stable team members for the last two years of the project, participating fully and making important contributions. Among their activities were attendance at a regional workshop, assistance with evaluation of a pilot seminar, public relations activities with the student senate and campus newsletter, and development of a slide show describing the seminar program. One of the students earned psychology field experience credit for assisting the coordinator with the evaluation of the program and supervision of the student assistants.

The president of Trinity College attended team meetings during Phases One and Two and stayed informed of later developments. Her role as a link with other Project QUE campuses kept the team in touch with some developments elsewhere. The dean provided very active support by attending team meetings, staying in communication with the coordinator, maintaining connections with the Council of Independent Colleges, foreseeing difficulties, and helping to create solutions.

Midway through the project, it became important to ask the assistant academic dean to serve as a team member. Her major responsibilities at that time were advising and faculty development. Her commitment and cooperation were valuable in implementing the seminar programs. Some other faculty and staff members, who either approached the team or were sought out by it, were important resources: in particular, the director of student activities, who had a strong interest in working with freshmen and knowledge of programs for freshmen at other institutions, and a member of the education department faculty with expertise in student development and peer-assistant programs. In addition, the seminar instructors brought their own expertise and enthusiasm to the program and helped to shape it.

The coordinator's role was an essential and many-sided one, involving the maintenance of communication among people on campus and with Project QUE staff in Washington, D.C., as well as organizing, motivating, and delegating. As a social scientist, this coordinator brought some evaluation research skills to the job, and, in the absence of an institutional research office, the evaluation effort remained almost entirely in the coordinator's hands. "Hindsight," according to the coordinator, "suggests the need for the effort and expertise of [people other than] the coordinator to ensure effective evaluation" (p. 4).

The campus team and coordinator kept in touch with the faculty through occasional memos and regular progress reports at faculty meetings. Two of the five department chairpersons at Trinity College were campus team members, and a third chair taught one of the pilot seminars. Thus, the team had other direct channels of communication with faculty members and ways to maintain faculty involvement. The dean served as an important communication channel with the administration. Communication with students received less attention, but the activities of student team members were helpful in this regard.

The project coordinator suggested that "the one campus group we should have involved in more structured ways was student life personnel. Fortunately, our Student Activities Director sought us out and initiated her involvement'' (p. 3). The campus team experienced no active resistance to the seminar program: ''The prevailing faculty attitudes have varied from enthusiastic involvement to passive acceptance ('Fine, you go fix up the freshmen before they get into my courses'), and the administration has been watchfully supportive. Our major difficulty in program development involved the loss of momentum that occurred when the first campus coordinator left and was not replaced for a year'' (p. 3).

This case study points to the particular value of including major college or university administrators on the initial planning committee, as well as the value of including students and of linking with key campus leaders (especially with regard to pilot testing particular program elements). As the project coordinator mentioned, one must be careful about asking team members to assume major responsibility for program evaluation, since this can often lead to conflict of interest, unless the team member is specifically and exclusively responsible for program evaluation during his or her tenure on the campus team. This case also points to the often forgotten liaison work with campus leaders from outside the academic area in which the target program resides. The dean of student services, director of development, vice-president for finance, or director of institutional research often can provide valuable assistance in terms of both advice and material resources.

Step Two: Establishing Program Selection Procedures

- *Responsibilities*
  The planning committee establishes the procedure in consultation with other campus leaders.
- *Tasks to Be Accomplished*
  1. Identify personal goals/expectations of planning committee members.
  2. Identify central institutional needs and problems as they relate to this project.
  3. Identify goals and objectives for the target academic program selection procedures.
  4. Identify campus resources, events, problems, and potentials as they relate to accomplishment of program selection goals and objectives.

5. Identify the strategy for program selection, assign responsibility for implementation of the strategy, and determine the schedule for program selection.
6. Consider factors that will ensure continued interest in and support for the target program selection procedures by members of the planning committee.

The planning committee must address a set of issues concerning the procedures to be employed in selecting an academic program for high quality development in Phases Two, Three, and Four. These issues could be addressed during two or three meetings of the committee on campus. However, as a number of college and university leaders who participated in the Strategies for Change and Knowledge Utilization project (Lindquist, 1978b) learned, these short meetings (held once or even twice a week on campus) are not nearly as effective or efficient as longer, less frequent, off-campus meetings. Of the many lessons learned from the large-scale strategies project—which was funded by the National Institute of Mental Health—this was one of the more mundane yet valuable. As one participant remarked: "One two-day retreat accomplished more than a whole year of two-hour meetings" (Lindquist, 1978b, p. 95).

Building on the strategies findings, Project QUE planning committees were encouraged to hold two-day planning meetings soon after the team had been selected. In developing a specific agenda to begin organizing and planning for Phase One, each planning committee can expect to face a unique set of circumstances and needs. A number of general issues, however, are appropriate for the agenda of most planning committees:

Personal Goals

1. Why is each of us, as a member of the planning committee, involved in this project?
2. How do our reasons for involvement apply to the tasks of this team?
3. What are individual expectations concerning problems and potentials for this planning committee?

4. For each member of the planning committee to find work with this team personally gratifying, what would have to be accomplished before the completion of its task?

Institutional Needs and Problems

1. What are the current unmet needs of this college or university?
2. How do these needs relate to selecting an academic program for highest quality development?
3. What are the central problems currently confronting this college or university?
4. How do these problems relate to selecting an academic program for highest quality development?

Project Goals

1. Realistically, what should be the goals of this project?
2. What should be the short-term goals of this project for the academic year?
3. By the end of Phase One, how might this project, if successful, tangibly benefit this college or university?

Helping and Hindering Forces

1. What forces (resources, events, problems, potentials) are currently operating in this institution that will or can aid in the accomplishment of the goals of this project?
2. What factors will or can hinder the accomplishment of these goals?
3. How can the negative forces be decreased, discouraged, or isolated?
4. How can the positive forces be increased, encouraged, or reinforced?

Cross-Project Impact

1. What other projects now or soon to be operating in this institution will help or hinder the successful accomplishment of this project?
2. How can these projects be of greater mutual benefit and/or of less mutual hindrance to each other?

Project Planning

1. Given the goals of the project and analyses of current and potential conditions at this institution during this academic year, how might procedures best be structured to assure reasonable agreement on the selection of an academic program?
2. What would be the best strategy for accomplishing the goals of the planning committee?
3. Who should assume specific responsibility for each step and aspect of project participation on this campus?
4. How will the team know and be assured that each assignment is successfully carried out?
5. What are a reasonable time schedule and sequence of events for successful completion of this project?

Team Functioning

1. What do we, as members of a committee that has assumed major responsibility for this task, do to ensure that our own interests in and support for the project are sustained?
2. How do we preserve good working relationships among the members of the team?

Step Three: Presenting the Program
Selection Procedure to the Campus Community

*   *Responsibilities*
    The planning committee designs and conducts the first community meeting.
*   *Tasks to Be Accomplished*
    1. Present the overview of the project and outcomes of the planning committee's meetings.
    2. Solicit general community reactions to the project and outcomes of planning committee meetings.
    3. Review general community reactions to the project and the planning committee.

Two sets of activities should be considered by a committee in beginning the process of building support for a new or revised program. In a small college, support must be built throughout the institution. In larger colleges and universities, support must be built in that part of the institution that is directly or indirectly affected by the proposed change. In a large institution, this might be the faculty in a particular department, students who are majoring in the program(s) offered by this department, and key administrators in the division or college in which this department is located. In building this support, the planning committee should first hold a community meeting to communicate the selection procedure established in step two. This meeting need be only one or two hours in length; it typically includes a presentation about the project and the program selection procedures to the community. To ensure full participation by the community in the selection procedure, those present might be divided into small groups of five to seven participants and asked to address the following questions: (1) What are your reactions to the program selection procedure the committee has chosen? (2) What advice or suggestions do you have for the planning committee as it sets about this task?

Although a regular faculty meeting was used by many Project QUE colleges to discuss the selection procedure, a community meeting is recommended to develop broader-based support and help ensure full participation by the community (not just the faculty) in the selection procedure. Furthermore, in most faculty meetings, "innovative" discussion methods—such as the meeting of participants in small groups—are rarely appropriate. In one particular case (Columbia Union College), however, it should be noted that the regular faculty meeting was used quite effectively in the program selection process (see Case Study Three).

CASE STUDY THREE
Columbia Union College
Takoma Park, Maryland

Target Academic Program: Cooperative Education
Primary Source: Klimes (1983)

On December 13, 1979, the president of Columbia Union College announced the college's intention to participate in Project QUE and introduced the QUE project coordinator. The president assigned seven members to work on the project as a planning committee. The first meeting of the planning committee, where it discussed the overview of the QUE program, convened on January 14, 1980.

First Community Meeting. During the January 17 faculty meeting, the faculty was briefed on Project QUE and requested to submit existing or proposed programs that might be developed into a quality program for Columbia Union College. There were thirty-two responses from faculty and staff. As a follow-up for those who did not respond because they had not attended the faculty meeting or because of insufficient information, another memorandum was sent through inter-college mail. It contained additional information about the QUE project and a request for suggestions for a target academic program. After telephone calls and some footwork, sixty-two people responded with fifty-five suggested programs that could be developed by the QUE project. These program suggestions were then organized according to subject areas, with the number of people suggesting similar programs also being noted.

Consultant from Project QUE Office. To gain an impartial perspective and to receive outside expertise as to successful programs in other small colleges, the planning committee invited members of the Project QUE staff to meet with them on the campus on February 11. Keeping in mind the present status of the college—its mission and its goals, along with the seven indicators of quality listed in Chapter One—the planning committee reduced the list from fifty-five to seven. Three existing programs were selected: computer science, English writing, and the remedial program. Four new programs were also selected: cooperative education, an honors program, television and media, and Washington area studies.

Second Community Meeting. During the February 14 faculty meeting, the faculty received the list of seven candidates for the target academic program. The mission, goals, and descriptors of the college, along with a description of the seven indicators of quality, were read and discussed at length. Following the meeting, faculty members, student leaders, and board members were requested to rank the seven programs. The results of the survey were tabulated for the three different groups. Each of the three groups indicated that, among the seven programs, there was strongest support for the cooperative education program.

Final Choice. The planning committee met on February 25 and on March 3 to make the final decision as to the target academic program. Being assured of administrative support, the planning team selected cooperative education.

Once this first round of information collection and sharing has been completed, the planning committee meets to review the responses that members of the committee have received to its plans and to make whatever adjustments seem appropriate. Once this has been accomplished, the committee will be in an excellent position to begin the actual selection procedure.

Step Four: Identifying, Collecting, Analyzing, and Synthesizing Information About the Institution

- *Responsibilities*
  The planning committee identifies information that it needs in the selection process. One or two members of the committee, along with appropriate campus resources people, collect, and analyze this information.
- *Tasks to Be Accomplished*
  1. Identify institutional information that is now available to the college or university.
  2. Identify information that is needed in the selection process.
  3. Assign priorities for collection of information that is not now available but is needed.
  4. Determine means to collect high-priority information.
  5. Collect and analyze information about the institution.
  6. Synthesize old and new information about the institution; relate this information to selection issues.
  7. Prepare written and/or oral reports on the institutional information, tracing out the implications of the information for the program selection procedure.

Institutional research can play an important part in the successful completion of Phase One. The committee should consider systematically the information needed for selection of a target academic program and, if it is not available, make plans for obtaining it. In many instances, a planning committee will have to establish some priorities regarding the type of new information that will be of greatest use, since the committee will not be able to collect all of the new information that would be of value. Phase One is neither a long-range planning project nor an extensive institutional research effort. The planning committee should not undertake a massive new research project or become overwhelmed with the institutional research data that already exist.

The planning committee, in most instances, should be particularly concerned with data about the mission of the college or university. Since the academic program selected for highest quality development will have an impact on the educational quality and future of the college or university, it must be compatible with the central mission of the institution. Alternatively, the campus community must recognize fully that this program may alter the nature or scope of this mission, if the project is taken seriously and the steps outlined in this book are followed.

At Huntington College (Indiana), important institutional data and documents were already available during Phase One. Special attention was given in the selection process at Huntington to departmental enrollment data, student interest data from the admissions office, and the following documents: statement of mission, faith, and philosophy of education; a list of intellectual, physical, social, and religious objectives for the college; a resolution on academic concerns; a set of economic, financial, management, recruitment, student life, and faculty and academic planning assumptions; and the planning policies of the college.

Step Five: Identifying Program Alternatives

- *Responsibilities*
  The planning committee, in conjunction with other members of the campus community, produces a list of program alternatives.
- *Task to Be Accomplished*
  Generate and solicit a list of alternative program suggestions.

The task of the planning committee at this point is to identify a number of programs from three sources. First, the planning committee should identify candidates from among programs currently in existence at its institution. Second, the committee may wish to identify one or more new program ideas. With a clear understanding of institutional mission and goals, as well as the current status of the institution, a number of new curricular ideas are identified as potentially of value to the college or university. Third, the campus community at large is used as an important source of suggestions. In QUE colleges, a number of means were employed to obtain these suggestions. Written suggestions and proposals were often solicited during faculty, divisional, or departmental meetings. Committee members in some QUE colleges conducted interviews with campus leaders and spokespersons to elicit their ideas. Suggestions can also be collected by distributing a questionnaire to the campus community.

Although the mechanics of such an approach can become time consuming, this method holds the advantage of providing an avenue for everyone in the institution to have their say. At Huntington College, the entire community was encouraged to submit ideas through the luncheon series that the committee sponsored, through posted announcements, and through oral announcements made in classrooms throughout the college. In addition, committee members solicited suggestions informally as they circulated on campus.

Step Six: Screening the List of Program Alternatives

- *Responsibilities*
  Members of the planning committee plan and implement a questionnaire and meeting.
- *Tasks to Be Accomplished*
  1. Survey the campus community regarding preferences for target academic program alternatives.
  2. Formulate a second list of potential target program alternatives (eight–twelve items).
  3. Review planning committee programs with the campus community at a community meeting.
  4. Formulate a third list of potential target program alternatives (four–eight items) on the basis of discussions at the community meeting.

Once a campus planning committee prepares an initial list of academic program candidates, it should enlist campus community assistance in reducing the list to a manageable size of from four to eight alternatives for final program selection. This can be done through a two-step procedure involving the use of a questionnaire and second community meeting. The questionnaire lists the academic program alternatives that were identified in step five and asks respondents to rate each of the alternatives as to its potential for meeting important criteria determined by the committee through their work during steps two, three, and four.

The committee should not simply select those items with the highest ratings but should also look for items that are particularly controversial (high ratings by some people and low ratings by others). These latter academic program alternatives provide an important impetus for discussion at the community meeting. Even if not ultimately selected, these controversial program ideas may help to spark conversations that clarify the institution's curricular purposes and provide "dissident" factions on campus with an opportunity to be heard.

With the second list of potential target programs in hand, the planning committee convenes a second community meeting. In the case of several Project QUE institutions, the initial questionnaire was bypassed, and the committee moved directly to the second community meeting. The Huntington College planning committee made use of its own judgment and the frequency with which various program suggestions were made during step five in deriving a list of six high-priority candidates for primary consideration at the second community meeting. The other suggestions that had been derived from the committee's interviews and conversations were also listed. The entire list was distributed to the college community with an announcement of the second community meeting.

The participants in the community meeting should be given copies of the second list of academic program alternatives and asked to address such questions as:

1. Which of the program alternatives seems to promote most effectively the central mission of this institution?

2. Which of the program alternatives seems to promote most effectively the primary goals (short and long term) of this institution?
3. Realistically, which of the program alternatives can this institution expect to undertake during the next three years?
4. Which of the program alternatives makes most effective use of the strengths of this institution?
5. Which of the program alternatives most effectively avoids the weaknesses of this institution or helps to overcome these weaknesses?

At this point, planning committee members should not be arguing for specific program alternatives themselves but should, instead, be primarily concerned with obtaining a clear understanding of the reasons given by various members of the campus community for supporting the selection of specific target program alternatives. The community meeting concludes with a request that each participant rank order the academic program alternatives that have been presented to them at the meeting.

At this point in the Phase One process, some colleges and universities may find one high-priority program. The planning committee in this case can move directly to step eight of Phase One and on to Phase Two. Many other colleges and universities (especially larger institutions) will have reduced the list at this point but not arrived at a single program alternative. The planning committee, however, will have accumulated a considerable amount of information, both from its own research and deliberations and from the responses of the community at large. This information provides an excellent base for the final selection of one program for high quality development.

Step Seven: Choosing a Target
Program for High Quality Development

• *Responsibilities*
The planning committee, in collaboration with campus leaders, makes the final selection of an academic program.

- *Tasks to Be Accomplished*
  1. Select an academic program for high quality development.
  2. Convey the decision and the rationale for the decision to the campus community.

As mentioned above, in some instances, institutional agreement has already been reached at this point in the planning process regarding the academic program to be developed in Phases Two, Three, Four, and Five. The weight of institutional research, the momentum and needs of the institution, and the events and resources present in the college or university may point clearly to a single program alternative. When this is the case, the planning committee should draw together the evidence supporting the academic program and move to step eight.

On the other hand, it may be that several academic programs will remain as potential candidates for selection. Each may have a degree of support on campus, and each may seem to be responsive to a variety of institutional needs and problems. Various factions on campus may be pressuring for a specific program alternative and arguing its value to the institution. If this is the case, the planning committee is faced with the difficult and sensitive task of making a choice among several viable alternatives.

The committee must develop its own criteria for selecting a program. One set of criteria found by many QUE colleges to be an excellent starting point for their own discussion was enumerated in Chapter One. By these criteria, such a program should be attractive, beneficial, congruent, distinctive, effective, functional, and growth producing. In addition, the criteria of penetration (potential depth of impact) and enablement (potential breadth of impact) were described and supported. These seven primary criteria were used quite successfully by the planning committee at Oakland City College (Indiana) in selecting its core curricular reform as the target academic program. These criteria were also used in its selection of the specific core courses that were to receive primary attention (see Case Study Four).

CASE STUDY FOUR
Oakland City College
Oakland City, Indiana

Target Academic Program: General Education
Primary Source: Pendergrass (1982)

In the selection of courses for their general education program, the faculty at Oakland City College made use of the seven criteria of quality that were defined by the Project QUE staff: that the program should be attractive, beneficial, congruent, distinctive, effective, functional, and growth producing. They first focused on courses that they thought would be *attractive* to potential students because of a unique integration of disciplines; for example, "Culture and Man's Behavior" (psychology, sociology, and anthropology) and "Fine Arts and the Modern World" (music, art, and history).

How could they know that these courses would be attractive? Market surveys might have been helpful to Oakland City College at this point, as they would for any other college or university that is tackling a large-scale program that will serve as a potential drawing card for many students. Will this new program draw in new students, while also drawing students who currently are attracted to the college? Is this new program compatible with the current image held by potential students at this college or university? If the new program offers a radical departure from tradition, then the people who are recruiting for this institution will not be able to build on its current image in the community. Rather, they will have to construct an entirely new image, which is a difficult if not impossible task.

Second, the Oakland City College faculty selected courses that they thought would be *beneficial:* "providing skills, knowledge and attitudes needed to function as an adult in the current era and be responsive to the environment, self, society and God" (p. 2). Under this criterion, they highlighted the courses being developed in the areas of speech and English composition, as well as courses that integrate philosophy and ethics (for example, "Philosophy and Contemporary Values"). Perhaps most importantly, these faculty members viewed benefit in terms of the specific goals and distinctive character of their own church-related college. Other colleges and universities should also define benefit in a specific and distinctive manner, in keeping with their own tradition and mission.

With regard to *congruence*, the planning committee at Oakland City considered the target academic program "consistent with the overall mission of the College as defined by the Board of Trustees" (p. 2). Furthermore, each course that was developed under Project QUE was to have "objectives stated in terms of student learning outcomes which [were] congruent with institutional objectives and student needs." While such procedures do not guarantee that the actual teaching and learning that occur are congruent with the stated objectives of the course, let alone the stated mission of the college, they do "prime the pump" for more intensive review of actual performance and outcomes in the classroom.

The criterion of *distinctiveness* was employed by Oakland City College faculty members in determining that their general education program should be not only integrative but also carefully balanced among the humanities, the mathematical and natural sciences, and the social and behavioral sciences. The general education curriculum that existed at the college when the QUE project began could not "guarantee such balance because of its elective nature." The faculty were quite right in describing this goal, if accomplished, as distinctive, for very few general education programs achieve an effective balance among these different perspectives.

With regard to the criterion of *effectiveness*, the measurement of desirable change in the students was an essential ingredient of the Oakland City College QUE project. The Comprehensive Outcome Measures Program (COMP) tests of the American College Testing Service were used to assess long-term progress in student learning. Skills, knowledge, and attitudes were also measured through traditional course evaluations and faculty observations. These various assessments comprised the means by which the Oakland City College faculty determined the level of effectiveness of the new target academic program. While other QUE colleges made even more extensive and sophisticated use of standard and unique student learning outcome assessment tools, the Oakland City College approach exemplifies the way in which program effectiveness can be operationalized, without an excessive outlay of time or money for extensive outcome assessment.

The quality of academic programs as defined by their *functional* characteristics was set forth at Oakland City College in terms of the students' acquisition of those specific skills, knowledge, and attitudes that are necessary "to function as good citizens." The general objectives of the new curriculum and student learning outcomes for each course at Oakland City are stated in terms of learning to prepare oneself to function in the modern world.

The final criterion of quality, that the program be *growth producing*, is employed at Oakland City in its expectations concerning cognitive, affective, and psychomotor development among students participating in the new core program. "A balanced, interactive, dynamic, innovative, producing and integrative student is the goal of the program" (p. 3). Future longitudinal studies after graduation will be initiated to measure the growth of students as related to the goals and objectives of the new QUE curriculum. These lofty expectations are commendable, especially if backed up by adequate professional development training for faculty, adequate time for program planning, and adequate administrative and clerical support to make the new general education program a reality.

One tool that may be of assistance to the planning committee in making this difficult decision is cross-impact analysis (Bergquist and Armstrong, 1985). This technique establishes as a selection criterion a program's capacity to have a positive effect on one or more of the other final program alternatives—thus reinforcing the importance of "enablement" as a criterion of program quality. The cross-impact procedure and the accompanying emphasis on enablement may help to break a deadlock in deliberations concerning final program selection, for they allow members of the planning committee to acknowledge the ultimate value of each of the final program alternatives, while selecting the one alternative that is valuable not only in and of itself but also as a vehicle for enabling other program alternatives to get started, to improve, or to move toward completion. Cross-impact analysis yields ratings of enablement while encouraging members of the planning committee to identify the extent to which various program efforts help or hinder one another.

The concept of enablement and the cross-impact analysis that can be used to introduce this concept into the program selection process are of value not only in breaking logjams in program selection deliberations but also in helping the planning committee to foresee and hopefully avoid interprogram competition and disruption. Several Project QUE colleges reported that interprogram competition was a major problem that their campus teams confronted when implementing the target academic program. Competition existed over the availability of resources for program planning and development, over the amount of attention and support given to the competing programs by key campus leaders, and over the allegiance shown to each program by faculty, students, and administration. At St. Joseph's College, for instance, an abundance of resources actually became a problem for the Project QUE team, for interprogram competition existed (St. Joseph's College, 1983). The target academic program at St. Joseph's focused on the improvement of an existing four-year interdisciplinary core program through faculty development. A grant from a major national foundation supplemented Project QUE. The college, however, also received several other grants for different in-service faculty development activities. One such grant was in progress at the beginning of the QUE project. Another grant was administered during the second and third years of the QUE project. Conflicting calendars and different in-service projects involving many of the same faculty members competed for the energies of the faculty and dissipated their concentration on the QUE project. "There were times," according to the project director, "when some faculty were unsure which project they were involved in at a given time" (St. Joseph's College, 1983, p. 1).

If a cross-impact analysis had been done at St. Joseph's during Phase One, then these problems might have been anticipated or even alleviated. The planning committee might have chosen to undertake another project that was not potentially distracting to the existing or anticipated faculty development projects. A project might have been formulated, for instance, that involved other segments of the college community, such as student advisement. Alternatively, the planning committee might still have selected the interdisciplinary faculty development project, but would have better coordinated and even integrated the three different faculty development initiatives.

On the more positive side, numerous examples can be offered of QUE projects having a positive and enabling effect on other programs. At the College of St. Teresa in Winona, Minnesota, a senior member of the Department of Education listed nine specific ways in which the college's target academic program (a liberal studies program) had had positive impact on the teacher education program at the college (Pirkl and Orlett, 1983). Similarly, faculty members in English and theater arts at St. Teresa, as well as the campus pastor, all identified major ways in which the target program has been of benefit to their own program.

Once the planning committee has decided which academic program will be planned and implemented during the remainder of the planning project, that decision must be conveyed to the larger campus community. The planning committee may wish to hold a third community meeting or informal discussions with key campus leaders or governance bodies. During these informal discussions or community meetings, committee members should communicate the procedures they followed in reaching their decision, as well as the rationale for the final choice that has been made.

Step Eight: Documenting Phase One Activities and Decisions

* *Responsibilities*
  The project coordinator prepares a summary of the activities and decisions of Phase One to be used in planning for Phases Two, Three, and Four.
* *Tasks to Be Accomplished*
  1. Document the procedures used to select the target academic program.
  2. Accumulate institutionally based evidence for selection of the target program, with particular reference to the mission, goals, and current status of the college or university.

The final responsibility of the Phase One planning committee and, in particular, the project coordinator is to provide a bridge to Phase Two, when membership on the committee may change to reflect the focus of the target academic program that was selected during Phase One. The procedures, outcomes, and, most important, assembled information from Phase One may prove to be valuable to the committee as it enters Phase Two. A considerable amount of effort can be wasted in subsequent phases if adequate attention is not given to documenting the important work from Phase One.

꙰꙰꙰ **4** ꙰꙰꙰

Determining Desirable
Program Outcomes

Phase Two involves identifying outcomes that lead to planning and designing a preliminary program (Phase Three) that will be tested and refined (Phase Four) and implemented (Phase Five). Evaluation should be integrated into all phases, though we will specifically address evaluation issues in our discussion of Phase Five.

Some committees may be particularly concerned about the amount of time required to give adequate consideration to key issues (for example, specific student learning outcomes or an intended program of evaluation) before proceeding with the initial implementation of the program. In response to these concerns, we would note that program planners often spend a great deal of time tinkering with the program after it has begun because they have not spent sufficient time planning prior to initiating the program. Each committee is urged to give serious consideration to the value of each step that is described in this chapter and to weigh carefully the consequences of bypassing any specific step or activity. Committee members are urged to answer the question: In an attempt to save time at this point in the planning process, are we adding time at a later point?

Step One: Reviewing the Composition of the
Planning Committee and Designating the Coordinator

- *Responsibilities*
  The committee (including the dean or academic vice-president and the president) considers appointment of

people to the planning committee and 'the coordinator's
position.

* *Tasks to be Accomplished*
    1. Review needs of committee membership and the coor-
        dinator role in view of the target academic program
        selected during Phase One.
    2. Affirm current membership or make substitutions or
        additions as deemed appropriate.

As a first step in program planning and design, it is
necessary for each college or unit of a university to reconsider
the composition of the planning committee. Often the nature
of the program to be designed necessitates the assignment of
different people to the committee and selection of a new coordinator. In Project QUE, in many instances, even though the
original QUE coordinator did not possess specialized expertise
in the area of the selected program, that coordinator was retained because, for example, he or she was highly respected in
the campus community and was viewed as someone who would
bring excellent facilitation skills and an important objective
perspective to the planning process. Similarly, even if the program primarily involved one department, one or two faculty
from other areas often were included on the committee to pre-
vent the program from becoming departmental rather than institutional. Most QUE programs affected several areas of the
college, so the inclusion of faculty from other departments
seemed appropriate. In larger universities, broader represen-
tation may be less appropriate—though the "enablement" dimension of the program planning process should be kept in
mind.

Many, but not all, QUE college planning committees included students. The chief academic officer continued to serve
on the committee, as did the president, at most QUE colleges.
In most instances, the president became less active in committee activities, instead working behind the scenes to procure adequate resources, build campus support, and keep board members
appraised of the program's progress.

One of the more elaborate approaches to planning was

devised by Huntington College (Indiana), which used three sub-committees: (1) a curricular planning group to work through the design steps for the academic portion of its program; (2) a cocurricular planning group to design important student activity components; and (3) an "input-evaluation" group for suggesting improvements and designing evaluation procedures. Barry University (Florida) also made use of the subcommittee approach, asking one group to define needs and desired outcomes for its written and oral communications program for high-risk students, a second group to have some preliminary discussion of an ideal program, and a third group to assess institutional forces and resources that could affect the program.

At King's College (Pennsylvania), the QUE team membership included administrators and faculty members who were also members of the college's planning/budgeting committee. According to the project coordinator (Farmer, 1981, p. 7): "This provided linkage between the planning directions set forth by the College and the research and design work of the QUE team. It also provided specific feedback into the deliberations of the planning/budget committee regarding review of institutional organization and structures, future personnel needs and desired allocation of resources." Other Project QUE colleges ran into major problems when assigning either program selection or program design to a standing committee of the college. While the planning committee at King's College apparently was able to effectively blend political and rational approaches to program planning, planning committees at other colleges and universities are likely to find the rational approach submerged in campus politics. In many state universities, for instance, rational planning models take a back seat to union-management issues or to "cross-cultural" conflicts between faculty situated in different and isolated academic departments. There really is no rational basis for deciding whether a psychological perspective in some contemporary social issues courses is "more important" than a political perspective. Similarly, when academic planning issues must be related directly to negotiated faculty loads and rights, there is little room for open, rational reflection by either faculty or academic administrators.

Step Two: Planning Phase Two Activities
for Development of the Target Academic Program

- *Responsibilities*
  The committee determines goals, strategies, and a schedule in conjunction with other campus leaders.
- *Tasks to Be Accomplished*
  1.   Determine what needs to be accomplished.
  2.   Determine how the committee can design and plan the academic program so that it is satisfying to members of the committee as well as other campus constituencies and it will lead to the accomplishment of all project goals.
  3.   Set a realistic schedule for the initiation and completion of events and accomplishment of results.

In embarking on the demanding process of designing an academic program, it is necessary first for planning committees to carefully define the goals, strategies, and schedules for this undertaking. During several initial meetings of the committee or, preferably, during a day-long retreat, three central questions should be addressed:

1.   *Goals:* What must be accomplished in terms of events, products, and project results?
2.   *Strategies:* How can these events, products, and results be achieved in a manner that is satisfying to members of the team, as well as to most campus constituencies?
3.   *Schedule:* What is a realistic schedule for initiation and completion of these events, products, and results?

Goals. The project goals for the year should be stated explicitly, so that all members of the committee, as well as others on campus, can know whether the goals are being achieved. Explicit responsibility for completion of each goal also should be assigned: (1) To whom will people look if this goal is not met? (2) Should this person be responsible for accomplishment of this goal? (3) If not, who should be responsible, and how can this responsibility be publicly acknowledged?

Strategies. Having defined goals and responsibilities, a planning committee should map out a strategy that takes into account three concerns: accomplishment of the task, satisfaction of all committee members with the procedures and expected accomplishments of the committee, and satisfaction of campus constituencies with the procedures and expected outcomes. In planning for effective task accomplishment, the committee first should identify the resources that are available for Phase Two: (1) Which people will be able to work on the project? (2) Which people have appropriate expertise and competencies to assist in the design? (3) Which people have sufficient interest and energy? (4) Which individuals or groups should be recruited for at least peripheral involvement in this project, even if their involvement is needed only to build campus support and influence the attitudes of specific campus constituencies?

The student body is often a valuable but overlooked resource for an academic planning project. Can one or more bright and highly motivated students be given some academic credit for assisting in the design of the program? A student can benefit greatly by serving as a research or administrative assistant to the project. Community resource people may be able to assist the project on a voluntary basis. Alumni may similarly be of service.

In addition to people, the committee should survey the physical and financial resources that are needed for this planning effort: (1) What kind of media (equipment, technical expertise) are needed and available? (2) Will the library, computer, housing, or food services be needed? (3) What about office space, typewriters, and file cabinets?

Developing a strategy for program planning activities for Phase Two should include a discussion by the committee about the way in which it will proceed. In conjunction with this concern, committee members should address the following questions: (1) How are we going to make decisions as a committee? Under which conditions will decisions be made in a different way (for example, might a decision concerning minor expenditures be made unilaterally by the project coordinator)? (2) When there are differences of opinion, differing expectations, or different goals, how will these differences be resolved? Who has the final word? Why? (3) How are we going to make effective use of appropriate expertise that is available on this committee? on this campus? off campus? (4) How do we encourage creativity, risk taking, and openness on this committee, without ignoring realism and responsibility? (5) How do we keep others on campus informed of our work and progress? How do we make sure that we involve all those who should or want to be involved as the design of the program develops? Often, when a new group begins to work toward the accomplishment of a specific task, it ignores these questions or assumes that the answers will emerge as it goes along. Several publications of the Council of Independent Colleges (One Dupont Circle, Suite 320, Washington, D.C. 20036) may be of value to campus committees when these questions are being addressed: *A Handbook for Faculty Development, Volume 1* (Bergquist and Phillips, 1975, chaps. 8, 9, and 10) and Volume 2 (Bergquist and Phillips, 1977, chaps. 8 and 9); *Handbook for College Administration* (Sprunger and Bergquist, 1978, chaps. 5 and 7); *Consultation in Higher Education* (Pilon and Bergquist, 1979, chaps. 2 and 3).

Several procedures and tools are recommended for balancing off ownership of the project by committee and various campus constituencies. First, it is often valuable for a committee to plan its activities in conjunction with (or at least in full awareness of) other major program initiatives on campus. One of the easiest ways to lose on-campus support for a project is to plan a program while ignoring other ongoing or developing programs. If the project is seen as "stepping on" other projects (as a result of schedule conflicts, distracted attention of campus leaders at certain times, and so on), animosity may soon develop. Inter-project conflicts can be avoided or at least reduced by developing strategies for the inclusion in the planning process of people involved in other major on-campus projects. This strategy may involve occasional joint meetings of the project committees, weekly or biweekly informal discussions between project heads, or a formal joint planning of project schedules.

At William Jewell College (Missouri), three major projects were under way at the same time: a general education reform project, development of a new tutorial program, and Project

QUE (computer literacy). Coordination meetings among the president, the dean, and the coordinators of the three programs were held in early fall and late spring in an effort to enhance communication, mutual planning, and support among the programs. In addition, each program coordinator was assigned membership on the college Curriculum and Educational Policy Committee. Participation on this committee has provided the major means for communication and dissemination of information regarding the target academic program to the college community.

An increased sense of campus ownership for the project also can be encouraged by involving the college or university community (or at least major sectors of it) in decision making at several key points in the planning process: selection (Phase One), design (Phase Three), and evaluation (Phases Four and Five). If the procedures recommended for Phase One (Chapter Three) are followed, there will be a precedent for community meetings in conjunction with the project. Several of the key decisions for Phase Two—for example, definition of outcomes for the program (step three)—can be made effectively in a group setting. If people in the college or university community can understand and "get hold" of the project, they are more likely to feel a sense of ownership for it.

Scheduling. The third initial task to be completed by the committee is the scheduling of activities. This scheduling should achieve three important results: clear expectations regarding deadlines for specific events and products; a realistic timetable for planning activities, so that responsibilities can be assigned legitimately and equitably; and sensitivity to the relationship between program planning activities and activities of other on-campus projects. Three procedures are recommended to accomplish these results: Gantt charting, the Critical Path Method (CPM), and the Program Evaluation and Review Technique (PERT) (Bergquist and Armstrong, 1985). These procedures are used extensively in many corporations and are taught in many basic courses on management. Taken together, these three procedures require a planner to consider the length of time that is needed to complete a set of activities, the appropriate sequencing of these activities, and the costs and benefits associated with various planning and implementation strategies. These procedures reduce the probability that time lines will be unrealistic, that delays in key events will thwart the entire project, and that project activities will disrupt other campus events.

Step Three: Defining Outcomes for the Program

- *Responsibilities*
  The committee identifies needs and outcomes in consultation with various campus constituencies.
- *Tasks to Be Accomplished*
  1. Assess current student, institutional, and societal needs as they apply to student learning in the target academic program.
  2. a. Identify high-priority needs that are closely related to the target program and to the current concerns of the college or university.
     b. Identify high-priority needs that exhibit low-cost/high-benefit potential.
  3. Write need statements that identify the source and nature of the need in unambiguous terms.
  4. Translate the need statements into statements of student learning outcomes.

Identifying Needs. Starting in Phase One, the most important task facing a college or university is identifying needs and ensuring that these needs define the priorities and content of the target academic program. At this point in the design process, the assessment of needs must be conducted with greater precision and focus than during Phase One, for the need statements are to be translated into statements of societal, institutional, and student learning outcomes, with particular emphasis on the latter. The outcome statements, in turn, will define the structure and content of the academic program and serve as a basis for its evaluation. As noted in Chapter One, the quality of an academic program should often be defined not only by the type and amount of resources that are put into the program but also by the outcomes of the program—especially to the extent that these outcomes can be specifically attributed to the program itself (the so-called "value-added" dimension of program quality).

A need can be defined as a discrepancy between a current state and some desired state. All problem solving and planning require the identification of salient information about the current state (situation), the clarification of the desired state (target), and the generation of alternative ideas (proposals) about how to move from the current to the desired state. To the extent that the situation and target are different from one another, the needs of the institution or specific academic program can be considered great; to the extent that there are no differences, then the needs can be considered minimal.

Need assessment always represents a *balanced* search for the current (situation) and the ideal (target) state of the institution or program. Too great an emphasis on the ideal leads to unrealistic planning. Too great an emphasis on the current status leads to mundane planning or lack of initiative. In keeping with this dual emphasis, any need statement should encompass descriptions of both the current and ideal states. To say that a college "needs a new general education program" may be sufficient to set general education as a high priority to be given considerable attention as a target academic program. However, once this area has been selected for attention, a more detailed analysis of the need for general education must be completed. What is the current status of general education at this college or university? What are the existing strengths and resources of this program? Who supports it? Why? One must analyze the strengths of the existing state so that they may be built upon. What do people see as the ideal—as the best possible program?

At this third step in Phase Two, a tentative statement can be made about both current and ideal states. The statement should speak to the nature of both states and the discrepancy between the two. A need statement regarding general education might read: "The current general education program offers a two-hour segment on technology, science, and values, which is often treated by students as irrelevant, superficial, and boring.

Students have indicated a need for a longer segment on this topic that is updated frequently and that represents the opinions of both science and nonscience faculty.'' This statement indicates the current and ideal length for the technology, science, and values segment and the current assessment and ideal image of students concerning the segment. There is sufficient detail to provide a committee with some ideas about how to design a program that is responsive to this need. This need statement serves as the basis for the committee's construction of an ideal design and collection of information about the current status during Phase Three.

At Marymount Manhattan College (New York), the Project QUE planning committee identified three major needs that related to their target academic program (computer literacy). Each of these needs was described with reference to a current and a desired state (Rich, 1983, p. 2):

A. *Current State*—About 98% of students at Marymount Manhattan College are computer illiterate.

A1. *Desired State*—To increase levels of computer literacy by 20% each academic year.

B. *Current State*—There exists a substantial computer anxiety which may be an off-shoot of math anxiety particularly evident among women students.

B1. *Desired State*—Reduction of this anxiety.

C. *Current State*—A substantial number of faculty are not computer literate.

C1. *Desired State*—To raise the level of computer literacy among faculty so that they can employ computer instruction in courses throughout the six divisions of the College.

While the Project QUE committee at Marymount Manhattan seemed to focus their attention on the current state and left the desired state a bit too ambiguous (with the exception of need C), they took an important first step toward clearly articulating a set of needs and had even begun to move toward formulating a strategy for meeting these needs (in this case, reducing computer-related anxiety). One needs to be careful, however, about leaving desired states open-ended. In the case of Marymount Manhattan's statements, one might wonder for how many years (in desired state A1) computer literacy will continue to increase by 20 percent. Conversely, a planning committee is encouraged, as Marymount Manhattan did in their third (C) set of statements, to trace out second-level desired states (for example, "employ computer instruction in courses") as well as first-level states (for example, "raise the level of computer literacy among faculty"). By drawing out some of the implications or anticipated spin-offs of a desired state, a planning committee can make a need statement even more persuasive, while also providing additional information that can be used in formulating strategies for addressing this need.

In formulating need statements, a committee should examine three different facets: students, the institution, and society. Ultimately, need statements that are derived from each of the latter two sources must relate back to the learning needs of students. Institutional survival is self-serving if it is not ultimately geared to a sense that this survival will benefit students. Similarly, only through the learning of students can a college make long-term, distinctive contributions to society. The following is a brief list of needs for each of these three sources:

Student Needs

1. Generic (basic) skills, knowledge, and attitudes
2. Prerequisite skills, knowledge, and attitudes
3. Personal skills, knowledge, and attitudes
4. Developmental skills, knowledge, and attitudes
5. Career-oriented skills, knowledge, and attitudes
6. Lifelong learning skills, knowledge, and attitudes

Institutional Needs

1. Achievement or maintenance of educational quality
2. Financial resources

3.   Marketing
4.   Stabilization and continuity
5.   Community support

Societal Needs

1.   Current
2.   Probable (future)
3.   Desirable (future)

Having identified a potentially large pool of need statements at the student, institutional, and societal levels, a planning committee is faced with the difficult task of being selective and establishing priorities: which needs are going to be given greatest weight? On what sources of information about needs will the committee rely? There are obviously no simple answers to these questions, for they involve human values and commitments. We suggest several criteria, however, by which decisions might be made concerning the priority to be assigned to specific needs.

First, needs should be assessed specifically with reference to the target academic program. One need may be of general importance for this college or university but better served by other campus programs. Another need may be of lower overall priority yet be so intimately connected to the target academic program that it is given greater consideration. Data already should be available concerning needs as related to the academic program, for in selecting this program during Phase One, the team engaged in rather extensive "soul searching." The information on institutional needs that was collected during step two of Phase One and the reactions to these need statements at the first community meeting (step three of Phase One) can be helpful, as can institutional information collected during step four of Phase One.

After members of the committee have reviewed this information, they may wish to update it, tailor it more specifically to the target academic program, collect additional information that relates specifically to this program, and organize this information in a way that can readily be translated into need statements. A variety of methods can be used to collect new or more focused information on academic program needs. Interviews can be conducted and questionnaires can be distributed to students, parents, faculty, administrators, and community representatives regarding academic program needs. The Project QUE committee at William Jewell College (Missouri) concluded that student computer literacy would be accomplished only after faculty became acquainted with the computer. They decided, therefore, to survey faculty with a questionnaire to determine their current level of knowledge about computers and their accompanying need for more education. Missouri Baptist College also made use of a questionnaire, sent to alumni and local corporations, in assessing needs for its business administration program.

At Trinity College (Vermont), the Project QUE planning committee decided to assess current students rather than either faculty or alumni, since their target academic program concerned small, personalized advising seminars for traditional-aged entering freshmen. A student needs assessment instrument was developed during the fall of 1981 and administered to 147 students at Trinity. Each student was to consider nine academic/cognitive and nine personal/affective "abilities or qualities, or kinds of help, that beginning college students may need." They ranked each of these nine needs from most to least important and indicated whether an advising seminar could help to meet each need.

In addition to collecting information from their own institution and/or surrounding community, members of the planning committee might survey comparable programs at other institutions to determine which needs seem to be met by these programs, which needs do not seem to be met, and the extent to which the relative success or failure of these programs relates to meeting or failing to meet certain needs. This procedure is particularly appropriate for colleges and universities that are in consortial arrangements, where there must also be some sensitivity to the development of competing programs. Project QUE was ideally designed for this interinstitutional comparison. At each of a number of yearly regional workshops, members of plan-

ning committees from ten to twenty QUE colleges from throughout a geographical region of the United States met to compare
notes as well as to learn about academic planning. Jack Lindquist has found that this ''cosmopolitan'' perspective on other
collegiate institutions and programs is a major ingredient in the
successful implementation of academic change programs at many
different kinds of collegiate institutions (Lindquist, 1978b).

The second and related set of criteria for establishing the
priorities of specific needs involves a comparison between needs,
on the one hand, and the current concerns and mission of the
college or university, on the other hand. Would meeting a particular need further the mission of the institution? Does the need
relate to currently pressing problems on the campus? Do many
people express an interest in this need? Rather than focusing
on the weaknesses of the institution, a planning committee can
focus on its strengths by comparing the need statement to the
mission of the institution or by looking at past successes of the
college or university. A committee, for instance, might identify five to ten exemplary recent graduates of the college or
university who have been affiliated with a program similar or
analogous to the target academic program and who have benefited most substantially and directly from experiences at the institution. The exemplary graduates are not necessarily those who
have been most successful at graduation or after graduation,
for many of these students would have been successful regardless
of the collegiate institution they attended or the program area
in which they were enrolled. The committee then identifies those
needs of the exemplary graduates that have been met by the
institution or program area. The exemplary graduates and people close to them (family, friends, colleagues, employers, faculty,
administrators) should be interviewed with reference to these
needs. While collecting this information, a committee also might
wish to determine which activities, conditions, or events contributed most to the success. This information can be of value
in the subsequent design of the academic program.

In comparing a need and the institutional mission of a
college or university, three actions are required. First, the committee should review current institutional mission and goal

statements for the area in which the academic program will be housed. Second, they should respond to the following questions: What would the general, overarching goals of a program be if they were responsive to the needs that have been identified? (moving from need to goal). What student, institutional, and/or societal needs seem to be most immediately addressed by the mission statement of the institution or program area? (moving from goal to need). Third, comparison should be made between the answers to these two questions. Which need statements correspond to, complement, or expand on the mission statement of the institution? These need statements should be given highest priority. Do the remaining need statements suggest that the current mission statement of the college or university should in some sense be modified?

Another mode of establishing priorities for needs builds on cost-benefit analysis. What would be the cost of meeting this specific need in terms of time, money, personnel, raised expectations, and so forth? What would be the cost of ignoring it? Which is the greater cost? (While one can only approximate the cost at this preliminary stage, such considerations may be important.) What would be the benefit of meeting this specific need? What would be the benefit, if any, of not meeting this need (other than avoiding certain costs)? These costs and benefits should all be weighed, particularly when difficult decisions must be made concerning the priorities to be assigned to specific needs (Palola and others, 1975).

Formulating Need Statements. Taking these several criteria for assessing priorities into account, the committee now should be ready to identify five to ten needs that will be central to the academic program being developed. These broadly defined needs then must be articulated as specific need statements that can be translated, in turn, into student learning outcomes. The need statements should indicate the sources of the need (student, institution, society) and the nature of the discrepancy that defines the need.

Typically, a committee is fairly clear about either the current (situation) or the desired (target) state. Usually, the first factor (current) receives more attention. Many teams will identify and discuss needs primarily with reference to what is wrong with the current condition. Emphasis will be placed on the description and analysis of current problems faced by students, by the college or university, and/or by society. In these instances, the "realistic" mode of program planning dominates either "idealism" or "activism," and the team is in need of a good dose of "pragmatism." For these committees, attention must turn to a more detailed description and analysis of a desired alternative state (the target). The following questions can be helpful in this regard: (1) If you could change the present situation with reference to this need, what would you want to accomplish? (2) What is missing in the present situation that you want? (3) What would be the desired outcomes associated with improvement in the current situation?

For those committees that have focused on the desired state (goals, hopes—the target), "idealism" becomes prevalent. Not enough attention is paid to the current situation. When committee members spend too much time dreaming about the way things could be, the following questions might be helpful: (1) In what ways does the present situation fall short of the goal, of the desired outcomes, of the ideal? (2) Why does the present situation fall short of the goal, desired outcome, or ideal? (3) What forces for improvement are there for reaching the desired state? (4) What obstacles stand in the way of reaching the desired state?

Having clarified both the current and desired states in a need statement, the committee is prepared to write clear and specific need statements. Clarity and specificity can be achieved by use of unambiguous terms. Phrases such as "does not understand how to," "needs to develop an appreciation for," "lacks knowledge of," "is unaware of," "does not develop a feeling for," and "has failed to acquire a familiarity with" should be avoided. Discrepancies should instead be described through use of phrases with unambiguous action verbs, such as: "cannot define," "is unable to distinguish between," "cannot identify," "cannot recall," and "does not recognize." Even rather subtle or complex needs can be described with action verbs and phrases, such as "(cannot) give in own words," "illustrate," "prepare," "read," "represent," "change," "rephrase," "restate," "interpret," "reorder," "rearrange," "differentiate," "make," "draw," "explain," "compare," "apply," "demonstrate," "estimate," "infer," "conclude," "predict," or "extend." Following are several examples of need statements that meet the criteria just articulated:

1. Students at this college currently do not have access to an adequate sequence of courses on accounting that will prepare them effectively for a career in this field. Students need a sequence of courses that will enable them to identify and apply basic principles of accounting (student-based need).
2. Our college currently is operating on a $75,000 budget in the fine arts department. In order for this department to operate a program that will enable students to produce professional-quality work, it needs a $100,000 budget (institutional need).
3. Our region faces serious ecological problems that threaten its economic vitality. Graduates need to be able to identify, describe, and contribute to the solution of the basic ecological problems of this region (societal-based need).

Identifying Desirable Student Learning Outcomes. Having articulated clear and specific need statements, a committee is ready to translate them into statements of student learning outcomes. This is done by first transforming the component of the need statement that relates to a desired state into a statement of desired student learning. In the case of student-based needs, this transformation may not be needed or may involve changing only one or two words. In the case of institutional or societal need statements, the committee should ask: What type of student learning will result if this institutional or societal need is met? What type of student learning must occur for this institutional or societal need to be met? A statement of student learning can be formulated on the basis of answers to one or both of the questions. The three need statements listed above might be reformulated as outcome statements about desired student learning in the following manner:

1. Students at this college will be able to identify and apply basic principles of accounting.
2. Students at this college will be able to produce professional-quality work in the fine arts department.
3. Graduates of this college will be able to identify, describe, and propose adequate alternative solutions to the ecological problems of this region.

As one can see, if the need statements are carefully articulated, minimal change is required to derive statements of desired student learning outcomes.

Writing Student Learning Outcome Statements. A clear, useful, and verifiable statement of student learning outcomes should contain at least three and possibly four ingredients (Cook, 1978, p. 41). First, the statement should specify *the learner.* Second, it should describe an *unambiguous and observable action* or an observable product of an action that will result from successful initiation (or completion) of the target academic program, as this action or product relates to the student in question. In *Developing Learning Outcomes*, J. Marvin Cook (1978) emphasizes the need for action verbs in student outcome statements. A third possible ingredient in a student outcome statement is *specification of conditions under which these outcomes will be assessed.* This is optional, for in some instances a committee may not want to specify any conditions at this early point in the design process or might not want to restrict the assessment of outcomes to a specific set of materials or specific testing environment. A statement of desired learning outcomes need not refer to when or how the learning outcome was acquired. It need refer only to the end point—the point of assessment. Finally, an outcome statement should contain *a description of the minimal level of acceptable response.* The statement should contain a milestone indicating when a student has attained an acceptable standard, so that the student might be said to have achieved a specific outcome and/or so that the student might be allowed to progress to some other level of learning.

In establishing standards, a planning committee must address several difficult questions: Do standards necessarily have to be quantitative in nature? Can standards be established on the basis of qualitative judgments made by acknowledged experts in the field? A planning committee will have to address these questions from its own perspective and philosophy of education and assessment. Our own recommendation is that levels of acceptable response should be stated in terms as explicit as possible. Quantification is desirable if the outcome is not distorted or made trivial by quantitative specification. Qualitative assessment is often more appropriate. Listed below are modifications of the three need statements that were generated above. Each of these statements now conveys information about desired student learning outcomes and meets the four outcome statement criteria that were suggested by Cook:

1. Students who have completed the new sequence of accounting courses will be able to identify and apply at least eight of the ten basic principles of accounting that have been articulated by the National Association of Accountants when presented with this task in an oral interview setting; ability will be judged by one or more accounting instructors.
2. Before graduating from the Department of Art at this college, all majors will have planned and initiated at least one exhibit of their work, received critical assessment of this exhibit from at least two members of the department, and replied to each of these critics with a detailed discussion of points made by the critic.
3. On a regional environmental problem-solving test prepared by faculty at this college in conjunction with three regional environmental protection agencies, candidates for graduation from this college will have generated a set of solutions to the problems that are presented and will have provided a written rationale for the solutions presented that is found to be satisfactory by a panel of three experts selected by the regional environmental protection agencies.

An interesting set of student learning outcome statements was prepared by Illinois Benedictine College for its Project QUE scholars program in a slightly different manner from that suggested above (see Exhibit 1). The Illinois Benedictine committee first formulated a set of learning objectives that indicated what a student in the program should be able to demonstrate. The committee then identified the standards of performance for each of these objectives and the means by which each objective would be assessed. While some of the objectives that this committee identified are somewhat ambiguous by Cook's (1978) standards (for example, "understanding of"), the standards of performance are quite specific, for in each instance they are based on the successful completion of a certain course or set of courses. The tools for assessing completion of these courses are quite clear in some instances, though unclear in other instances (for example, "course requirements"). Many QUE colleges specified successful course completion as the primary criterion for achieving a certain student learning outcome; however, they were still left with the task of determining how a student has successfully completed the course. Troublesome issues associated with standards and modes of assessment are only deferred by specifying course completion as the primary criterion for accomplishing a student learning outcome—they are not resolved.

There are several different ways in which the need statements can be translated into student learning outcomes. One or more members of the planning team who are particularly proficient in working with outcome statements might take on the task. Alternatively, the entire committee might be given the task, so that everyone is fully aware of the rationale behind the learning outcomes that are formulated. At the College of St. Teresa (Minnesota), the QUE planning committee chose the latter approach (see Case Study Five).

CASE STUDY FIVE
College of St. Teresa
Winona, Minnesota

Target Academic Program: Design for Choicemakers (Core
                            Curriculum)
Primary Source: Battaglini (1983)

"Imagine, if you will," notes Dennis Battaglini at the College of St. Teresa, "the following scenario as a faculty member is about

Exhibit 1. Student Learning Outcome Statements; Illinois Benedictine College, Lisle, Illinois.

Objectives (General Learning Outcomes)	Scholars Program Standard of Performance	Assessment	Assessor
The student should be able to demonstrate:	Completion of:		
• Superior ability to perceive, analyze, think, write, and speak	• Freshman colloquia; scholars courses	Course requirements; portfolio	Instructor Portfolio Committee
• Reading and speaking proficiency in a second language	• Foreign-language courses; year abroad	Course requirements; standardized foreign-language test; portfolio	Instructor Portfolio Committee
• Understanding of the mutual relationships and interdependence of peoples and nations	• Core courses; scholars courses; year abroad	Course requirements; standardized ETS pretest and post-test; portfolio	Instructor Portfolio Committee Mentor
• Understanding of leadership theory and of communication and group process skills and an ability to use them effectively	• Scholars courses; activities	Course requirements; participation in community agencies, projects, and so on; portfolio	Instructor Portfolio Committee
• Knowledge and appreciation of the religious, philosophical, scientific, literary, and artistic heritage of human civilization	• Scholars courses; core courses, activities; year abroad	Course requirements; participation in cultural activities, projects, and so on; portfolio	Instructor Portfolio Committee Mentor
• An ability to identify and analyze moral issues and to come to informed decisions in the presence of conflicting issues	• Scholars courses; core courses; activities	Course requirements; participation in activities; portfolio	Instructor Portfolio Committee Mentor
• Understanding of the methodologies of the social and natural sciences and of the impact they have on the world	• Scholars courses; core courses	Course requirements; portfolio	Instructor Portfolio Committee Mentor
• Understanding and appreciation of human creative expression	• Scholars courses; core courses; activities	Course requirements; participation in activities, projects, and so on; portfolio	Instructor Portfolio Committee Mentor

Notes: 1. Freshman colloquia and scholars courses use the writing standards developed by faculty to assess ability to write at superior level.
2. Course syllabi exhibit specific learning outcomes (objectives) to measure attainment of general learning outcomes.
3. Mentors should be involved in developing/assessing portfolios.

Source: Kittel (1982).

to embark on teaching a completely new course for freshmen'' (p. 1). The faculty member is told that this new course will allow him to ''flex'' his creativity, to teach content of substantial merit, and to receive the help of one or more colleagues in a team effort. Furthermore, through grant funds, the college will provide paid planning time to the instructor during the summer to create and write the course. He went on to note that:

> For some instructors, this sounds quite attractive. After you have made a commitment to teach the course, you are given the following additional information:
>
> - A representative group of faculty has listed a rather large set of general objectives for you to use as outcomes for your course.
> - The objectives are disjunct and vague.
> - Some of the objectives are ''co-curricular'', i.e. they cross the barriers that formerly existed between academic affairs, student affairs, and pastoral affairs.
> - Persons of the three areas above have very serious interest in seeing that ''their'' objectives are met by your instruction.
> - You and the other members of the team have two weeks to write detailed syllabi including measurable objectives, teaching strategies, and plans for division of labor within teams.
> - No one text book seems to fit the subject matter of your course.
> - Furthermore, in the workshops, no immediate and general consensus is reached on what the common elements of the course should be.
> - Finally, you are told that your class and other sections will participate in an external evaluation on the chosen objectives [p. 2].

This is the situation that nine faculty at St. Teresa faced in the beginning stages of course planning during the summer of 1982. At their first meeting, the team of instructors classified a comprehensive list of thirty-five objectives (given to the team by the QUE committee) into four major categories: critical thinking, value clarification, modes of knowledge, and career/life planning. The sorting that occurred enabled the planning group to begin the difficult task of writing a course that at the time seemed viable but unclear. According to Battaglini: "Everyone seemed to have a different idea as to what these objectives meant. Thus, a great amount of necessary philosophical conversation was spent on hearing each other's viewpoint. . . . Although the instructors used the better part of three days in an open forum on the subject, from that point on we started to accelerate the concretization of our objectives. We also found that by using critical thinking as the major goal category, we would "use" the other objectives as a means to that end" (p. 2).

The planning group next addressed the issue of assessment. How do we measure critical thinking? They eventually turned to published and standardized tests. At this point, they struggled with the issue of "the tail wagging the dog" with regard to standard tests determining the criteria to be employed in assessing achievement of the program's objectives. "However," as Battaglini observed, "with the time constraints on the planning stage (two weeks), we found this to be an excellent and efficient way to begin writing meaningful and measurable objectives to which we would all try to adhere." He also noted that "one of the most valuable experiences we as a group had in those first two weeks was a newly gained knowledge (for some) of behavioral objectives. I would recommend strongly that, for a team of instructors writing a common set of course objectives, each of the members read a common set of guidelines outlining procedures for writing such objectives. This would certainly facilitate the actual writing process" (p. 3).

Battaglini offered several other valuable suggestions regarding this process: "Let the teaching faculty know beforehand what demands are going to be made of them in preparing for such a course. . . . Secondly, give the responsibility of objective writing to the entire institutional team rather than letting external groups decide what is best for a course they will not have to teach. This approach will insure that the characteristic of *practicality* as well as *validity* will more likely be addressed." At another point, he suggests that "one can plan in a more meaningful way with a blank calendar of days of the quarter 'staring' one in the face. It wasn't until a calendar was brought out that many of us started to push the pencil and get things done" (p. 4).

While this good advice might not be appropriate to all colleges and universities that are engaged in academic planning, Dennis Battaglini has identified several key guidelines in the identification of program outcomes or objectives: (1) use a standard, widely understood set of guidelines in formulating these outcomes, (2) build widespread ownership for the outcome formulation process and, as a result, the outcomes that are eventually selected, and (3) give those working on the task realistic expectations regarding the time needed to formulate the outcomes, as well as a firm deadline against which to operate.

A third approach is to bring in someone from elsewhere in the institution (for example, the department of education) who is an expert in the formulation of learning outcome statements. This has the advantage of broadening the base of involvement in the program but the disadvantage of making the final statements less accessible to or "owned" by members of the planning group. If possible, a hybrid approach is advised, whereby the committee does most of the work in formulating the outcome statements but these statements are reviewed and modified by other people on campus with expertise in student learning outcomes and/or by people on or off campus with little knowledge of the target academic program (to determine whether a "naive" reader can understand the nature and purpose of the outcome statements that have been formulated).

Once the student learning outcome statements have been formulated, it is advisable to summarize the work done during this third step of Phase Two by creating a table or list that contains the need statements and accompanying student learning outcomes. This table can serve as an excellent summary statement about the purposes of the target academic program—for use both on campus (communicating to faculty, administrators, and students) and off campus (communicating to alumni, community supporters, and potential funding sources). Brevity and specificity in the need and outcome statements are greatly appreciated by most nonacademics.

Why Student Learning Outcomes?. After drafting outcome statements, the committee is prepared to engage in the stimulating process of designing an ideal version of the target academic program. As mentioned above, this third step will enable most committees to gain a clearer sense of the current and desired states that relate to the program. This clarification will, in turn, help the committee to define more precisely the needs and outcomes of the program before its inception.

Academic planning is an iterative process, whereby desired outcomes (target) not only help to define program activities (proposal) but are themselves further clarified by the formulation of program plans. Nevertheless, if careful attention is given to the specification of learning outcomes at this early point in the design process, one can ensure (or at least maximize the probability) that the academic program will perform the functions for which it is designed and meet the most pressing needs of students, the institution, and society. Huntington College (Indiana), an institution that made extensive use of student learning outcomes, found new clarity of purpose and, in some instances, new perspectives from which to view old, unresolved problems. At Mary College (North Dakota), one of the original outcomes of their QUE project was developed because of the need to decrease the high attrition rate of "undecided" freshmen. They first translated this need into a student learning outcome statement: Ninety percent of all freshmen [participating in the QUE target program] will have made a tentative career choice by the end of the first semester. As the planning committee at Mary College began to trace out the implications of this outcome statement, they came to realize its limitations. The learning outcome was changed, and students were encouraged to spend more time deciding on and exploring various career choices. By clearly stating the anticipated learning outcomes for this program, the Mary College planning committee was able to correct and modify its basic assumptions about the program and, as a result, the design of the target program. When anticipated and desired outcomes are not made clear, many academic programs move in unanticipated or unintended directions.

The advantage of specifying student learning outcomes also lies, in part, in its emphasis on the systematic appraisal of new program ideas as they relate to specific, stated outcomes. The new core program at Seton Hill College, for instance, relies heavily on student learning outcomes. The stated outcomes of the program are constantly being addressed in the review of all new program ideas: "each year the Freshman Seminar Advisory Board invites faculty members to submit proposals for review for offerings as freshman seminars. Faculty members must show in their proposals how the course they intend to teach responds in detail to four major outcome areas. Once the course is selected as a core offering, the instructor consents to a process by which the course is reviewed and evaluated. . . . Changes are proposed for the seminars which could include modifying the outcomes (these change as student needs do), or reshaping the course. All proposed changes to outcomes are presented to the curriculum committee and the Academic Dean for review. As a result, several faculty members, accustomed to designing core courses based on outcomes, now are starting to redesign the other courses they teach as well'' (Boyle, 1983, p. 2).

The specification of student learning outcomes also has positive consequences for the student. The learner who knows what is to be accomplished is able to more effectively assist in this accomplishment. If an instructor lists the expected outcomes of a course in the syllabus, then the learner's very knowledge of what he or she can expect or hope to accomplish aids the learning process, promotes the achievement of the outcome, and, perhaps most importantly, helps the learner become more self-sufficient. Student learning outcomes enable the teacher and learner to openly work together on the joint enterprise of learning. The learning agenda of the instructor is no longer kept hidden: both the teacher and learner know what is to be learned, and both will be successful to the extent that the student has mastered what has been defined by the instructor. If the student knows the desired outcomes, then he or she can monitor progress toward these outcomes without always having to check with the instructor. This self-regulation enhances the maturation process and prepares the student for a future life in which this self-regulation is essential.

While viewed by the architects of Project QUE as the foundation of academic planning, the outcomes approach was one of the more controversial elements of the project. The crux of the challenge was aptly described by one campus coordinator (who chose to remain anonymous): ''The major shift to describing program goals in terms of student outcomes . . . required effort on the part of faculty, most of whom had conceptualized their teaching in terms of their content areas rather than with reference to student outcomes.''

This is where most campus team members started. While thinking in terms of the *results* of learning may not have gained total acceptance among the several hundred faculty and administrators who were eventually involved, we believe that most came to the conclusion summarized by reports from two of the campus teams. The leader of one campus team noted that: ''In terms of suggested changes in the planning process, most important for *not* changing would be the development of outcomes statements. Although in the beginning many of us were skeptical about the value of starting our work by developing outcome statements, I think we would all agree now that the outcomes statements have served to give us direction, and once we had determined where we wanted to go, helped us get there.'' Another campus team leader concluded that: ''The attitude of our faculty and staff to the outcomes approach has changed from 'should we do it?' or 'ignore it and maybe it will go away' to 'say, this has potential; show me how to do it.'''

✵✵ 5 ✵✵

Designing the Program
to Achieve Desired Outcomes

A curriculum planner or planning team will often immediately focus attention on designing a program that is ''realistic'' with reference to campus resources, traditions, and policies. While realism clearly is needed in the final design of a new academic program, it can hamper creativity when introduced too early in a curricular planning process. Many people who are experienced in course and curricular design suggest that an ''ideal'' design should be formulated first, followed by a consideration of resource limitations, traditions, and policies and a realistic reformulation of the design. Robert Diamond and his colleagues at the Center for Instructional Development of Syracuse University provide a rationale for this process (Diamond and others, 1975, pp. 41–42): ''The preliminary [design] should represent the best possible instructional sequence for meeting the specific goals of the student population. It should be, in effect, the *ideal*. Experience has shown that it is most efficient to start with the best possible program and then modify it according to the specific administrative, material, and human constraints that exist. Limiting the original design to meet anticipated constraints tends to reduce both its flexibility and quality and thus generate an inferior program. Another reason for trying to develop an optimum design is that many of the traditional restraints are unnecessary and, in some instances, are unreal. The final design will probably evolve slowly after many revisions as new data are provided and as various viewpoints are discussed until a final and acceptable form is reached.''

While it is easy to find reasons for not designing an ideal program, most Project QUE colleges that followed this route found their efforts rewarding. The project coordinator at Eureka College (McCoy, 1983, p. 6), for instance, noted that "one of the most important aspects of the [QUE] project for [Eureka College] was the emphasis placed upon determining what would be an 'ideal' program. As may be true at many institutions we are apt to think of program development simply in terms of 'tinkering' with already existing programs. Even though we were actually working with an already existing program, the challenge to think of an ideal program was beneficial."

A number of side benefits can accrue from an initial focus on the "ideal." Sometimes the Project QUE president was able to raise funds or the college was able to reallocate funds to make the ideal a reality. Several of the QUE institutions used the ideal plan for the new program to obtain outside funding (from government sources, such as Title III and the National Endowment for the Humanities, or from private sources, such as the Lilly Endowment and the Kellogg Foundation, smaller foundations, or individual donors in their area).

Step One: Designing an "Ideal" Target Academic Program

- *Responsibilities*
  The committee drafts the preliminary design, probably with the assistance of other constituencies (both on and off campus).
- *Tasks to Be Accomplished*
  1. Explore alternative ways in which the target academic program might be designed with reference to time, space, resources, organization, and procedures, so that this program might achieve the outcomes identified in Phase Two.
  2. Select a design for the target program that is desirable, appropriate, and feasible with reference to the program outcomes.
  3. Provide sufficient detail for the initial ideal program design such that the audience for this design might gain a clear sense of how it would "work."

Many strategies can be employed in designing an ideal program. One strategy that made extensive use of the student learning outcome statements was implemented by Seton Hill College (Pennsylvania), as described in Case Study Six. The one ingredient that is found in all effective strategies is the encouragement of individual initiative, original thinking, intuition, and risk-taking behavior. The design of an ideal program is of value only if a committee uses the occasion to be imaginative and even a bit playful with new images and ideas (Bergquist and Armstrong, 1985).

CASE STUDY SIX
Seton Hill College
Greensburg, Pennsylvania

Target Academic Program: Core Curriculum Renewal
Primary Source: Boyle (1982)

The Project QUE committee at Seton Hill College began its work on designing an ideal program for its core curriculum renewal project during the fall of 1981 by reviewing curriculum models that individuals or small groups of faculty members had designed to address the outcome statements that the committee had previously generated. According to the project coordinator, this "proved to be a mistake. Although the models which were presented were excellent, confronted with the entirety of a new configuration of core courses, committee members responded by counting credits in the disciplines. No matter how some members of the Committee tried to see the model as a response to the outcome statements, many more were looking for evidence that their disciplines retained at least the same account of credit-bearing recognition in the new core as they had in the old core" (p. 3).

The project coordinator suggested that the committee temporarily abandon the idea of looking at the whole curriculum model and, instead, design and develop a smaller element of the curriculum. The committee agreed to focus on a limited number of outcome statements and brainstorm responses to them. They selected the world-orientation group of outcome statements, focusing on content outcomes that had to do with the students' cultural heritage and with communication and integration skills. Before selecting an ideal design that was responsive to the world-orientation outcomes, the committee further refined these outcome statements and identified the resources that they might need in order to develop a course or program in light of the chosen outcomes. Committee members met in a brainstorming session, in which they listed all the ways it would be possible to achieve these outcomes. After ranking the ideas generated in that session and consulting by mail with the faculty who now teach in the core program regarding their present methods of achieving the outcomes, the committee selected a sequence of outcomes and a general outline for the program being developed.

The "ideal" design featured a hub course staffed by the college's most talented lecturers and a series of related satellite courses in the disciplines that would serve as discussion sections for the hub lecture series. The Western Cultural Tradition Sequence, as it was called, would be a two-semester, twelve-credit core requirement for sophomores. The project coordinator noted at this point in the design process that the committee, "in its efforts to devour and digest the whole curriculum, like the famous South African animal, the phalarope, which is said to consume itself in its burning desire to catch its own tail, almost succeeded in bringing about its own demise during this phase of its activities. Too ambitious a project can be a lot to swallow in one gulp. We learned to divide and conquer" (p. 4).

The committee then asked the academic dean at Seton Hill to meet with department heads to discuss the feasibility of their departments' supporting the proposed program for the fall of 1982. The committee also scheduled a meeting of the faculty where the ideal design could be presented and faculty could respond with suggestions for making it realizable. The committee asked the faculty by mail for suggestions regarding the content of the hub course and what primary texts they considered essential reading for such a sequence.

The committee collected faculty responses to the presentation of the new core sequence, and, with the advice and opinions of several coordinators of majors in which a large number of students were enrolled, they designed the "realistic" model of the Western Cultural Traditions Sequence. They also invited department and program chairs to schedule individual appointments with QUE committee members to discuss specific difficulties that their departments or programs might have with the new sequence of the core.

The campus coordinator and the coordinator of the freshman seminars at Seton Hill then met with the freshman class to discuss the planned changes in the core that would affect this group of students. The students expressed lively interest in the new core, some resistance to it, and a great deal of curiosity. While many suggested that the new core was a good idea, some also thought that the "next class should do it." Still others were excited about the prospect of doing things differently and being part of the experimental class. Give and take with students on issues of the curriculum proved to be a worthwhile and stimulating exercise, and the committee agreed to plan more sessions in which faculty members and students could meet to discuss core requirements.

Exploring Ideal Program Elements. Regardless of the methods used to generate new ideas and perspectives on the academic program, each committee should explore alternative elements in each of five different design dimensions: (1) time, (2) space, (3) resources, (4) organization, and (5) procedures (Bergquist, Gould, and Greenberg, 1981). The following questions suggest ways in which each of the five dimensions might be discussed by the planning committee while designing the ideal program:

Time

1. What should be the duration of the target academic program and of various elements in this program?
2. When should various elements of the program be initiated during the academic year?
3. How could this program use the twelve-month calendar?
4. When during the day and week should program activities be held?
5. To what extent can people who are active in this program (faculty, students, others) choose their own time to participate in it? What constraints or barriers do they face?

Space

1. Which aspects of the program should be held on campus? Which could be held off campus? Where?
2. Which aspects should be held in areas that are formally designated for instruction? Which could be held in noninstructional areas?
3. To what extent can the location of activities for this program readily be changed or made mobile?
4. To what extent can people who are actively involved in this program select their own space in which to participate?
5. What effect will the design and decor of this space have on the program?

Resources

1. How many and what kind of on-campus people are needed to staff this program? Off-campus people? What kinds of expertise are needed? Will some people need to learn new roles and skills?
2. To what extent can people who have not previously been extensively used at this institution be brought into the program as resources?
3. To what extent can participants in this program be resources to themselves and their peers?
4. In what ways might various media (print, TV, movies, slides, radio, and so on) or other technologies (computers, telephone, and so on) enhance this program?
5. What special resources from on or off campus can be brought in to enhance this program?
6. What financial resources are needed?

Organization

1. What should be the nature of the administrative unit that will implement and/or maintain this program? Where should this unit be housed in this college or university?
2. What should be the role of faculty, students, and administrators in the ongoing planning, management, and evaluation of this program?
3. How does this program relate to the student's major, minor, general education, electives, and/or degree requirements?
4. How does this program relate to other programs, offices, or units of this college or university?
5. How does this program relate to accrediting or licensing agencies and requirements?

Procedures

1. Will students receive academic credit for participation in this program? On what basis will the credit be granted? How will the work of students be evaluated—if evaluation is necessary?
2. What methods of teaching and learning will be employed?
3. In what way(s) will students be expected to learn in this program (alone, small group, experiential, and so on)? What are the implications for other design dimensions?
4. How will the program be monitored and improved?

Selecting an Ideal Design. The various program elements that are brought forth and discussed must eventually be evaluated, screened, and integrated for the committee to arrive at a specific ideal design. The seven criteria of quality (attractive, beneficial, congruent, distinctive, effective, functional, and growth producing) that were identified in Chapter One and that were suggested as criteria for the original selection of the target academic program (Phase One) are equally as appropriate for the selection of specific program elements. Each program element might be reviewed and evaluated with reference to each of these seven criteria. An overall assessment concerning the *desirability* of each program element can then be derived on the basis of this review.

While a specific program element must be desirable, it should also be *appropriate* to this specific program and *feasible* as a component of the program. A program element may be exciting and highly desirable yet not make sense in a particular institutional setting. Several of the questions that might be asked about the appropriateness of the program elements are: (1) Might this element more appropriately be housed in another department, division, or program unit on campus? (2) Are many of the probable outcomes of this program element irrelevant to the outcomes identified in Phase Two? (3) In view of this institution's mission, is this element more appropriate to another institution? If this program element were highly successful, would it be inclined to move this institution away from its established goals and mission? Would it be inclined to move this institution toward new and more appropriate goals?

In considering feasibility, the planning committee begins to move from the ideal to the realistic. Some program elements may be desirable and even appropriate yet not feasible, given current campus resources, the history of the institution, and/or current institutional priorities. At this point, the committee should be concerned only with screening out those program elements that clearly are not feasible. If there is any disagreement among committee members about the feasibility of a particular program element, it should be retained until additional information is collected concerning its feasibility during step two. Following are several questions that might be addressed in the committee's consideration of feasibility: (1) Are knowledgeable and skillful people currently or potentially available to initiate this program element? Can relevant knowledge and/or skills be acquired readily by people who are available and interested? (2) Are sufficient financial and appropriate physical resources (space, machines, materials, and so on) currently or potentially available to support this program element? (3) If this program element were initiated, would it receive sufficient institutional attention and support to survive an initial period of testing, review, and revision? In completing work on this initial ideal design for the target academic program, the committee should provide enough design detail to enable other people to get a sense of how the program would operate if initiated in its ideal form. In creating the design, a committee may choose to work for one or more hours over several weeks or more intensively over a shorter period of time.

A planning committee may find that it cannot effectively assess the desirability, appropriateness, or feasibility of program elements until these elements are fleshed out more fully. While some working out of details is desirable in some instances, the committee should not expend a great deal of time and energy at this point creating a highly detailed program design, for some of the program's basic structure may change when the committee takes the next two steps—collecting more institutional information that is pertinent to the program design and formulating a realistic academic program design.

Step Two: Assessing Resources, History, and Priorities of the Institution

- *Responsibilities*
  The committee collects and analyzes information in association with other campus leaders and, if available and appropriate, the director of institutional research.
- *Tasks to Be Accomplished*
  1. Collect information on the resources, history, and priorities of the college or university as they relate directly to the target academic program.

2. Analyze collected information with reference to positive and negative forces acting on the target academic program.

Throughout this book, a repeated cycle of reflection and action is recommended for effective planning. Academic programs often either lack sufficient thoughtful reflection or are stymied by an unwillingness to commit good ideas to action. Both reflection and action are essential, and at this point in the program development process, when a major action step—the design of a realistic program—is about to be taken, the committee should back off a bit to collect more information and reflect on its significance for the design of the target academic program.

Collecting Information

During step one, when the ideal program is being formulated, many questions will arise concerning feasibility, program acceptance, and/or probable program success. Several QUE colleges actually found that they needed to answer some questions before they even began the process of designing an "ideal" program. At King's College (Pennsylvania), for instance, rather extensive data collection about student needs preceded the design of a career/life planning program (see Case Study Seven).

CASE STUDY SEVEN
King's College
Wilkes-Barre Pennsylvania

Target Academic Program: Life Development/Career Education
                                          Program
Primary Source: Farmer (1981)

During Phase Three, the planning team at King's College first sought to determine student perceptions of life development/career education needs. The committee developed a short questionnaire to assess these needs, basing it on several published instruments in the field. They also administered the Astin Survey Instrument of the

Cooperative Institutional Research Program (University of California at Los Angeles) to all entering students at the college, beginning in September of 1981. Results from the latter instrument enabled the committee to compare student attitudes at King's College with those of a large national sample of students.

The planning committee also wanted to find out about faculty attitudes concerning career education. They administered a student career development instrument developed by McLean and Loree to all faculty during the spring of 1981. The results were analyzed on a division-by-division basis.

Third, the committee explored life development and career education programs at other institutions. Team members entered into discussions with program personnel at other colleges and universities, and several team members visited Ithaca College to review its program in this area.

Fourth, a faculty workshop was planned for the spring term of 1981 to promote faculty understanding of and sense of ownership for the proposed target program. This workshop focused on student needs, the role of effective advisement in student retention, and a preview of the emerging life development program. Emphasis was placed on the need for faculty to present their own expectations, concerns, and suggestions for the proposed program.

At this point, the planning committee began to design the "ideal" program. They reviewed the literature on existing career education programs and previous deliberations on career education at King's College, then began to build the ideal program, emphasizing effective linkages to existing student support services on campus and departmental faculty resources.

Finally, the planning committee moved on to the design of a realistic program. The ideal design was modified in accordance with the availability of personnel, collection of more extensive information relating to student perception of needs, evaluation of courses that were being pilot tested (Phase Four), further study of referral patterns among existing student support services, and determination of which faculty members in each department were willing to be trained as career resource people.

In their reorganization of the recommended Phase Three steps, the King's College planning committee was able to assemble an impressive wealth of information about the target academic program prior to design of the ideal program. This committee also built faculty ownership for the program by gaining their involvement prior to designing the ideal program. Many college or university committees might not wish to go through such elaborate steps. However, in King's College's case, faculty were going to be asked to perform new functions and develop new attitudes toward the education of students for future careers, so their active involvement was appropriate.

In some instances, the questions that arise are not "researchable"—that is to say, they essentially concern issues of values (for example, "Is this program really going to meet the most important needs of this university?" or "Wouldn't it be better to respond to the needs of this constituency before we serve the needs of that other one?") and cannot be answered simply by gathering additional information. Other questions that are raised, however, are "researchable": they *can* be answered with additional information. Questions of this type often concern (1) current or potential resources, (2) past history and anticipated trends, and (3) the priorities of specific constituencies. Each of these forms of institutional information should be collected and analyzed with specific reference to the target academic program.

In many instances, this step involves a review of data that are collected routinely by the institution, suggesting the involvement of the director of institutional research, if such a position exists on the campus. Alternatively, this step might be negotiated primarily by reviewing the data that were collected during Phase One or Two. In other instances, new information may have to be collected by the planning committee or by other people on campus—the director of institutional research, other campus committees or offices, or students who serve as staff to the committee and receive academic credit for this service.

Institutional Resources. Institutional information about resources will touch on several different areas (staff, students, other people, materials, money, facilities, time) and come from several different sources (campus records, archives, publications, accreditation reports, administrators, faculty, staff, students, alumni). Information should be collected that will enable the committee to answer the "researchable questions" that arose during the design of an ideal program. Some of the questions that typically arise are:

Staff

1. What faculty are available to assist with this program, and what are their strengths relative to both the content (subject matter, problem, and so on) and process (teaching, counseling, and so on) of this program?
2. How much faculty time can be committed to this program, and at what salary levels will participating faculty be supported?
3. If there is inadequate faculty support for this program (because of restrictions in time, money, interest, or expertise), are there procedures available to make more efficient use of existing resources (for example, increasing student-faculty ratio, using videotapes)?

Students

1. What are the average age, prior education, work experience, and/or skills of students who probably will be entering this program?
2. What are the probable attitudes of potential students about the structure and subject matter of this program?
3. What are the probable expectations and priorities of students who are likely to enter this program?
4. What are the probable short- and long-term goals of students who will be likely to enter this program?

Other People

1. Are there administrators, clerical staff, or other people on campus who have relevant knowledge and/or skills and are available for this program? Are institutional policies and precedents supportive of the use of these people?
2. Is appropriate support (expertise, time, money) available from off-campus people who are associated with the institution (alumni, spouses of faculty or administrators, trustees)?
3. Are there people off campus with relevant knowledge and/or skills who would be interested in assisting with this program? Are institutional policies and precedents supportive of the use of these people?

Materials

1. How might the college or university's library, museum, art gallery, performing arts center, and/or media center contribute to this program?
2. How might community resources (libraries, museums, schools, community agencies, and so on) be used for this program?
3. Are there precedence and money available for the acquisition of commercially available materials to support this program?

Facilities

1. How much on-campus space is available for this program, and what type? What are the capabilities of this space (seating, media, hours of availability)?
2. What kind of off-campus space is available for this program? What are the capabilities of this space?

Money

1. How much money is available for further design and development of this program?
2. How much money is available for implementation of this program?
3. What are the prospects of obtaining outside funding for this program (federal or state grants, grants from private foundations, donations, loans, and so on)?
4. What are the possibilities of new monies being made available from on-campus sources, as a result of either additional institutional revenues or budget reallocations?

Time

1. How much time is available for further development of this program? What deadlines must be met?
2. How often and for how long is this program expected to be in operation? How flexibly can time be treated in this program?

A committee may wish to assign each of its members to one or two of these areas or may wish to first see how many of these questions can be answered without the collection of additional information, then map out a strategy for the collection of additional information by members of the committee.

Past History and Anticipated Trends. A committee should be able to answer the following questions with information from within the institution: (1) Has there been a past attempt at this institution to initiate a program of this type? What were the outcomes of this initiative? What was learned from this initiative? (2) What have been the most important attempts at bringing about major program development at this institution in recent years? What was learned from these efforts that is relevant to the development of the target academic program? Often, some of the people on campus who have the most information about these questions are those who are resisting the development of the target academic program. We tend to use past history as a means of thwarting new program initiatives—"We tried that seven years ago and it didn't work"; "That's the way we used to do it!" These criticisms can become the basis for the collection of valuable information. The critics might be asked to be more specific about what happened seven years ago or about why the "old way" is no longer appropriate. One should ask the critics to be historical analysts for the project, so that the committee members can learn from the past, rather than repeating mistakes. While this strategy is not always appropriate, given the biased perspectives of many critics, it frequently is effective as a means of "constructive co-option," especially if members of the committee are sincerely interested in this analysis. Additional strategies for confronting "recalcitrant" critics of a new academic program can be found in the work of Everett Rogers (Rogers, 1983), Ronald Havelock (Havelock and others, 1971), and Jack Lindquist (Lindquist, 1978b).

Institutionally derived information about future trends should include quantitative projections from past and present institutional data (for example, projections of student enrollment or changes in the composition of student populations over the past five years). Quantitative projections that are based purely on trend extrapolations, however, are not always justified, given the occurrence of both predictable and unpredictable events and changing conditions. Scenario writing often is more appropriate, for several different descriptions of probable trends and future conditions can be sketched out (Bergquist and Armstrong, 1985). Alternatively, a modified Delphi technique (Bergquist and Armstrong, 1984) can be employed as a means of gaining broad institutional consensus about specific future trends. Given the rather time-consuming nature of a Delphi analysis, however, this method should be used only if future trends are particularly important in the design of the academic program or if a shortened Delphi technique is employed.

In addition to the specific history and trends of the college or university, a committee should be more broadly aware of the history and trends of American higher education and of the curricular area in which the academic program is being developed. Not every member of the committee needs this knowledge and perspective. However, someone on the committee should have it. Lessons learned at other colleges and universities about how to bring about new program development and curricular reform are particularly important. For this reason, one or more members of the team should read Jack Lindquist's *Strategies for Change* (Lindquist, 1978b). Lindquist provides an insightful and thoughtful description and analysis of program development and renewal at seven collegiate institutions. Progress and obstacles to change are reviewed. Many of the lessons learned in Lindquist's study also are summarized in his section of *Developing the College Curriculum* (Chickering and others, 1977). The work of Jerry Gaff with the General Education Models program during the early 1980s is also quite valuable in this regard (Gaff, 1981, 1983). It would be foolish for a committee to ignore the important, sometimes positive, sometimes painful, lessons that have been learned at other colleges and universities.

Institutional Priorities. In addition to institutional resources and history and general historical trends in American higher education, a committee should examine current institutional priorities to obtain an accurate picture of the probable support that the academic program will receive in the next year or two. Priorities can be determined by both work and deed. Key campus leaders might be interviewed concerning their current and future support for the program (as it is tentatively described in the ideal design of step one). This support would then be compared with support for and preoccupation with other current or future programs, events, conditions, and problems on campus. The actual decisions made and actions taken by these leaders also might be examined to determine the extent to which the verbalized support and statement of priorities seem to be reflected consistently in present action and projected budget allocations. Future priorities may differ from past priorities, yet statements of support should be tempered by past records of action and achievement.

Analyzing the Collected Information

Having collected institutional information on resources, history, and priorities, the committee is in a position to conduct an analysis with specific reference to the target academic program. A force-field analysis can be performed at this point. This analysis begins with the identification of forces (people, events, resources) that help (positive forces) and hinder (negative forces) successful achievement of the target program outcomes (Bergquist and Armstrong, 1985). The ideal design should be modified to increase the strength and resilience of positive forces and decrease the strength and resilience of negative forces. If there is a considerable lack of clarity, more information might have to be collected about specific forces prior to moving on to step three.

Step Three: Designing a Realistic Target
Academic Program to Meet Specified Outcomes

• *Responsibilities*
  The committee drafts the realistic design in consultation with other constituencies.

- *Tasks to Be Accomplished*
  1. Identify the implications of the force-field analysis (step two) for modification of the ideal academic program.
  2. Prepare a realistic design for the target academic program.

No one process can be recommended for the transformation of an ideal design into one that is realistic, for this transformation will differ greatly depending on the nature of the program being designed and the information collected during step two. The committee may wish to use the force-field analysis that was completed during the previous step to systematically re-examine the time, space, resources, organization, and procedures of the target academic program. The committee may even choose to review the outcomes identified during Phase Two, as part of the reiterative process of the Academic Planning Model. The committee then should carefully and systematically modify the ideal design of the target academic program to make it more realistic.

These actions might best be taken in conjunction with a broad campus constituency in order to extend ownership for the program that emerges from this design process. Broad-scale participation is particularly important at this step, because the product of this step will be initiated during Phase Four. Furthermore, even with extensive institutional research (step two), a target academic program can be made maximally realistic and appropriate if a number of different people are involved in the revision of the ideal. Large-scale group meetings should be avoided in the preparation of the ideal, for large groups often stifle creativity. At the stage of realism, however, ''the more, the better''—if the process is properly managed. Diverse and even conflicting perspectives can aid in polishing a program design.

The committee might hold a one- or two-day retreat and invite other campus leaders to join in on the task of designing the realistic target program. The previous work of the committee should be reviewed, with detailed attention being given to the ideal design and the information collected and force-field analysis conducted during step two. Participants should be reminded that they are being asked to work within the context of the outcomes that have already been carefully identified. It is not their task to question the basic premises or goals on which the program is based. If this understanding can be reached before the retreat begins, potential disruptions and hard feelings can be avoided.

After the committee's past work is reviewed, the participants spend several hours discussing the ideal design and force-field analysis and then break into smaller groups, with one or more members of the planning committee serving as recorder/facilitator in each group. Each group is assigned the task of examining a specific aspect of the program in more detail, given the ideal design and institutional information. The small groups then report on their deliberations, and a final general session is devoted to the formulation of a realistic design that incorporates recommendations from each of the small groups. The committee subsequently meets to polish this design.

Instead of a workshop, the committee might wish to use the campus mail to circulate a description of the ideal design and a summation of the force-field analysis. Recipients of this material are requested to submit their recommendations for changes in the ideal design given this force-field analysis, or to take exception with the analysis and suggest an alternative interpretation of the data that have been collected. The committee then reviews the recommendations and analyses that have been received and formulates a single, realistic design.

Looking Ahead

With the completion of the target academic program design, the committee is ready to move toward testing and implementation of this program—the primary activities of Phases Four and Five. If the Phase Three process that is described in this chapter has been followed, then most planning groups should find that they have designed a program that is of excellent quality, as well as being understood and supported by the academic community. Over the long run, perhaps the greatest benefit is derived from direct experience with and observation of a systematic planning process by the college or university community.

Many collegiate program planners rarely engage in careful design work. When one witnesses the effect of this work, in terms of both the quality of the program and the quality of support, then it becomes very hard to return to old ways of doing (or not doing) academic planning. As Rachel West (1983), the Project QUE coordinator at Marian College (Indiana), noted, "the teaching team [for Project QUE] believes that the process of designing the course has been advantageous not only to themselves and to the potential success of the pilot-test, but also to other members of the college community who . . . observed the process" (p. 2). A description of the design process that was used by the Marian College team is to be found in Case Study Eight.

CASE STUDY EIGHT
Marian College
Indianapolis, Indiana

Target Academic Program: Interdisciplinary Global Studies Program
Primary Source: West (1983)

In the early fall of 1980, the Project QUE campus team at Marian College discussed the critique of the target academic program proposal that was submitted at the conclusion of Phase One to the Project QUE office. In accord with suggestions made by readers of the proposal, the team decided to revise the proposed global history course to incorporate social science and religion in addition to history. It was apparent that such a course, entitled Global Studies, required a team of teachers representing the incorporated disciplines.

The team was composed of a coordinator, the professor who had previously designed the history course, and a member of the sociology department. At another meeting with the QUE campus team, the three instructors emphasized the point that, if the course was to succeed, it was imperative that members of the teaching team should mutually agree upon any other members selected for it. This principle was accepted. Accordingly, the teaching team asked that the head of the theology department complete their ranks.

The four members of the teaching team, the academic dean, and one other member of the campus team attended a regional curriculum planning conference in October 1980, where they formulated the primary student learning outcome for the course and became familiar with the process of arriving at such outcomes after assessment of student needs (step three of Phase Two). Shortly after returning to campus, the teaching team began meeting regularly (usually over lunch) to devise student learning outcomes based on institutional, community, societal, and student needs. This proved to be beneficial in terms of clarifying the focus of the course for members of the teaching team. It had become clear that what all were looking for in the course was a way to develop within Marian College students, most of whom come from rural and small-town Indiana, a broader appreciation of other peoples and other value systems, together with the ability to recognize the multiplicity and interrelatedness of factors shaping events, situations, and problems in today's world.

The team met for an entire day during Christmas vacation to discuss the content and a tentative outline for the proposed course, using the chronological framework of the previous course in global history. The focal theme of the course would be the concept of the "global ecumene" and its formation, a concept developed by the author of the text to be used during the course. The team decided that topical presentations should be done individually but that all members of the teaching team should be present as often as possible. Three days during each semester were designated "summation days," when the teaching team would discuss with students the basic themes of the time period covered during the preceding weeks; summation day would be followed by a test, partially essay and partially objective.

After a draft syllabus was completed, the team reviewed it and made some revisions. It was then forwarded to the Academic Affairs Committee and to the College Council for their consideration. Throughout the course of the year, the project coordinator reported to the College Council concerning the status of the proposed course, and council members became more fully acquainted with the concept and content of the student learning outcomes for this program. As a result, pilot testing of the course (Phase Four) was unanimously approved by the College Council in March 1981, with the provision that a task force be appointed to study current general education requirements of the college in light of introduction of the proposed course. In the weeks following approval of the pilot test, the teaching team refined the syllabus and prepared themselves to teach the course. Changes in the syllabus were made necessary by the departure of the head of theology from the college and the resultant necessity of assigning religious topics to guest lecturers.

Throughout this process, the Marian College teaching team paid careful attention to student learning outcomes and their continuing contact with campus leadership. They also allowed the design to be flexible initially, so that they could reconceive the course in broader terms, and were able to remain sufficiently open even at the end of Phase Three to accommodate the departure of a key member of the team from the college.

🎕🎕🎕 6 🎕🎕🎕

Pilot Testing, Reviewing, and Refining the Program

During recent years, many curricular changes have taken place at colleges and universities throughout North America—often with sizable support from foundation or government grants. Many of these curricular changes have failed to realize their potential because they were fully implemented without prior testing. These failures prompted the designers of Project QUE to include a pilot-test phase in an effort to enhance the chances of program success. To our knowledge, Project QUE is unique in this respect among national higher education projects. The actual experiences of Project QUE colleges seem to have justified this emphasis on pilot testing. Those colleges that took this phase of academic planning seriously found that the final implementation phase (Phase Five) was considerably less difficult and the final product of the academic planning process was of higher quality.

An assessment of the degree to which anticipated outcomes are achieved is critical to the usefulness of any pilot test—not only outcomes related to student learning but also those related to faculty and staff learning. If a pilot test is not systematically assessed, then its contribution to revision and refinement of the target academic program will be greatly reduced. Moreover, pilot testing a program—or some of its components—provides an opportunity to pilot test assessment instruments, designs, and methods to determine their feasibility for use in evaluating the program during its implementation phase.

As we look more specifically at some of the advantages of pilot testing a newly conceived or revised academic program,

105

several points become immediately apparent. First, pilot testing allows for the development of more skillful performance by faculty and staff and improvement of program organization and resources—all of which increase the probability of achieving the learning desired from the program. Pilot tests also enable a planning committee to avoid mistakes that would have an adverse effect on a large number of students and would, in turn, create antagonism toward the program. Such antagonism may have serious implications for student morale, recruitment, and retention, community relations, and institutional reputation. At the same time, a planning committee may miss opportunities for creativity, intellectual excitement, and appeal if risks are not taken. Pilot testing should encourage these risks and provide a vehicle for the evaluation of the desirability of their results.

We recommend a seven-step procedure to prepare for and initiate one or more pilot tests. As in the case of Phases One through Three, particular circumstances related to each campus and, more particularly, to each target academic program will dictate the extent to which these specific steps are to be followed.

Step One: Planning Phase Four Activities for Development of the Target Academic Program

- *Responsibilities*
  The committee determines goals, strategies, and schedule in conjunction with other campus leaders.
- *Tasks to Be Accomplished*
  1. Determine what has to be accomplished.
  2. Determine the ways in which the target academic program can continue to be designed and planned and/or can be pilot tested, assessed, and refined in a manner that is satisfying to members of the committee and other campus constituencies and that will lead to the accomplishment of project goals.
  3. Set a realistic schedule for the initiation and/or completion of events and results.

Determining What Has to Be Accomplished. By this point, the college or university has been engaged in the academic planning process for some time. The planners have acquired considerable experience in planning for the target academic program, as well as knowledge about their own academic community. As they embark on Phase Four, they may wish to reflect on their experiences to date and use this reflection in planning for Phase Four. The following questions might assist the planning committee in this reflective process:

General Questions

1. What have you found to be the most helpful resources (people, programs, equipment, policies) for promoting academic change? What have been the major barriers (people, programs, policies) to change?
2. What have been the critical incidents in determining the relative success of your planning of the target academic program to date? What have been the critical incidents that have prevented your academic program from being even more successfully planned to date?
3. If you were to start this project over again, how would you change (if at all) the way you have proceeded?

Specific Questions

1. What are the strengths and distinctive features of your target academic program? What excites you about it? What do you think does or will excite other people about it?
2. What are the current or potential weaknesses of your target academic program? About which part of the program are you most concerned? Which parts of the program will be hardest to ''sell'' to other people?
3. About which parts of your academic program do you feel confident? Why? Which parts need more work? Why?

Implications

1. In planning for Phase Four, how should the goals, strategies, and schedule of the project be changed to reflect what you

have learned to date about academic reform on your campus?
2.   How can you more effectively make use of the available resources and avoid or overcome the barriers to academic reform on your campus?
3.   What probably will be the critical incidents in the near future in determining the relative success or failure of your academic program? What can you do to anticipate these incidents in terms of capitalizing on those that will be beneficial and minimizing the impact of those that are likely to be disruptive?
4.   How do you reinforce the strengths and distinctive features and eliminate or isolate the weaknesses of your target academic program during Phase Four?
5.   What are the unanswered questions about your academic programs? How do you obtain the answers?

These questions are best addressed in a retreat setting by members of the committee, as well as other central actors in the target academic program. Once these participants have discussed their responses to some or all of the questions (or related questions that are uniquely suited to their target academic program), the committee should determine the goals, strategies, and schedule for Phase Four.

    In many instances, the Project QUE planning committees during Phase Four initiated a series of activities that built the resources (faculty, equipment, instructional materials) needed prior to full-scale implementation of the target academic program. The College of Notre Dame (Maryland), for instance, identified three sets of activities to be accomplished during Phase Four in its development of a "communications across the curriculum" program. The first two of these sets of activities move the planning committee directly toward the successful pilot testing of various components of the target academic program, while the third set helps an institution build a solid base of skills and knowledge among its faculty about how to teach communications skills in all segments of the curriculum.

    First, the College of Notre Dame's planning committee pilot tested an interdisciplinary math-English course called

"Mathemenglish" and a developmental English course with a writing lab. They also pilot tested three new courses, one each in drama, history, and psychology, redesigned to incorporate writing and speaking as methods for teaching content. Second, they assessed each of these pilot tests. Third, they pursued several faculty development efforts. A seminar was conducted by the chair of the English department for instructors in the pilot-test courses. Furthermore, two faculty members attended a regional workshop on "writing across the curriculum." Finally, a three-day workshop was held on campus between semesters, which reviewed the concepts of the "communications across the curriculum" program. This conference was attended by two-thirds of the faculty on a voluntary basis.

Some Project QUE colleges used the pilot tests primarily to resolve the fears and uncertainties that grew among some constituencies concerning the target academic program during Phase Three. The evaluators for the target academic program at the College of Notre Dame (Maryland), Jack Lindquist and Jill Tarule (1982), noted that "in the past [at this college], nothing got started unless everyone [faculty and administrators] agreed it would work" (p. 4). As a result, much of the discussion centered on the fears of faculty and administrators concerning the unknown and unproven. By using pilot tests to answer the questions and concerns of project skeptics at the College of Notre Dame, "the system of approval prior to testing has been reversed" (p. 4).

Similarly, at the College of Mount St. Joseph (Ohio), some faculty members expressed considerable skepticism about the ability of faculty outside the communication-oriented disciplines to teach effective communication to their students. While the careful design of a target course reduced some fears, "only a successful pilot [test] will convince those whose concern is with the use of faculty in areas other than communication. . . . It was the view of the QUE committee that a vote to institute the TAP as a requirement without piloting the whole program and evaluating the results first would jeopardize the program" (McPeak, 1983, pp. 2–3).

At Ohio Dominican College, by contrast, much of the fear seemed to reside among the students who would participate in the target academic program—a weekend college for adult students. According to the project coordinator at Ohio Dominican (Caspar, 1982, p. 1), the pilot test of the college allayed "the original fears on the part of WEC [weekend college] adults that they would be unable to perform successfully in these courses." At many Project QUE colleges, fears are now addressed by systematic testing of ideas rather than by either obsessive debate or politicking.

Determining Satisfactory Ways to Plan, Test, and Refine. The committee should now move toward formulation of a strategy for Phase Four that respects both the task requirements of the target academic program and the people needs of those working on or affected by the program. This point in Phase Four deliberations was particularly important for the planning committee at Illinois College, for this group used Phase Four not only to pilot test specific components of its Public Service Studies Program but also to test the specific way in which the target program was to be administered once it was in full-scale operation. The planning committee appointed a coordinating board consisting of faculty and students from several departments to develop and implement the pilot tests of its target academic program. The planning group, however, soon discovered that this board was too cumbersome to accomplish the tasks of either design or administration in an efficient manner. In the process of making this decision, the planning committee also concluded that the program envisioned was unwieldy. A more realistic design emerged, which focused on specific public service internship experience for students from a variety of majors, with the course requirements to be handled within each major. Thus, for Illinois College, the pilot-test phase was critical in designing a program that could actually be implemented, given financial and personnel constraints at the institution.

Developing a Realistic Schedule. Finally, the committee should formulate a schedule of activities for Phase Four. Scheduling may have to be much more flexible than was the case with previous phases. The exact number, duration, and nature of pilot tests cannot be specified at this initial stage, for each pilot test (or at least most of them) should be defined in part by the results of previous tests. Several optional plans might be drawn up that identify the scheduling implications of doing one, two, three, or four pilot tests of varying duration and magnitude.

Step Two: Identifying Components of the Target Academic Program to be Pilot Tested

- *Responsibilities*
  In consultation with other campus leaders, the planning committee identifies the components to be pilot tested.
- *Tasks to Be Accomplished*
  1. Identify those target academic program components about which there are researchable questions that can be answered at least in part through observation and assessment of their pilot implementation.
  2. Make a preliminary determination of which type of pilot test could answer these questions.
  3. Identify those academic program components that require further development of skills or knowledge or accumulation of experience among those people who are currently or potentially associated with the target academic program.
  4. Make a preliminary determination of which type of pilot test could provide the needed skills, knowledge, or experience.
  5. Establish a priority list of potential pilot-test projects on the basis of the relative importance of the questions, skills, knowledge, or experience and the potential costs (time, money, resources) associated with each possible pilot test.
  6. Depending on the constraints of time, money, and other resources, select one or more of these potential pilot tests for design and implementation.

There are two primary values of a pilot test to the planning of a new or revised program. First, one might find that even after the assessment step of Phase Three (step two) and after the development of a realistic academic program design, there are researchable questions that remain unanswered and that require the observation and assessment of some component of the program while it is in operation. Some questions will remain unresolved, either because they are not researchable (that is, they primarily involve the domain of values rather than of information) or because the planning process has left someone out or ignored someone's feelings.

Questions regarding priorities and paths to be taken often necessitate negotiation and compromise. Additional information that is gleaned from a pilot test on a particular program component will rarely change the mind of someone who does not value the outcomes of this particular component, nor will it gain the support of someone who was ignored when the decision was made to include this component or to do this pilot test. Nevertheless, in many instances, just as the aviation engineer must ultimately rely on a wind tunnel to answer certain complex questions about aeronautic design, so should an academic planner use a pilot test to provide answers to lingering questions about specific academic program components or the overall program design. At the College of Notre Dame (Maryland), for instance, lingering questions that were addressed in their pilot tests concerned: (1) Can faculty from disciplines other than English teach communication skills through content in their courses? (2) How can the teaching skills needed to do this be learned? Several pilot courses were conducted by non-English faculty at Notre Dame to see how they would do. Several different faculty development activities were also pilot tested to answer the second question, concerning prerequisite teaching skills. Most of the Notre Dame pilot tests were "course embedded"; that is, they were conducted within the context of existing courses.

A pilot test also provides a low-threat environment in which people who are to help conduct the target academic program can learn new skills, gain necessary knowledge, and acquire additional experience before engaging in the full-scale program. This kind of environment is rarely available to academicians yet is essential not only for their professional development but also for the benefit of students who will be participating in the program. Much as a novice airline pilot will first practice in the safe, though realistic, cockpit of a simulated aircraft and will first fly several planes without passengers and with guidance from an experienced pilot, so should an instructor who is teaching a new program or course, using a new method, and/or working with new colleagues be provided with a setting in which mistakes can be made, new skills and knowledge can be acquired, and alternative approaches can be tried at minimal cost to students or risk to the institution.

Identifying Components to Be Tested and Types of Tests to Be Used. Not all components of a target academic program will need to be rehearsed or tested in a pilot setting, for the operation of some of these components (for example, a lecture in one's own discipline) has already been mastered by the person responsible. Most components of target academic programs fall into this category. It is essential, however, that new or significantly modified components be identified and possibly subjected to pilot testing.

In many instances, all or a large portion of the target academic program was pilot tested by Project QUE colleges. Other Project QUE colleges, however, seemed to benefit greatly by focusing on very specific components of their target programs during the pilot-testing phase. The planning committee at Barry University (Florida), for instance, narrowed in on their target communication skills program by focusing their pilot test on specific aspects of the oral communications component of the program. They attended to the students' skill in the use of vowels and built a pilot referral program for training students in the use of this skill.

In establishing priorities for pilot testing, we suggest that committee members first identify researchable questions that still face them concerning specific components of the overall academic program. The committee then should make a preliminary determination of which type of pilot test might most directly and effectively answer each of these questions. Several different types of pilot tests are described later in this chapter.

The initial design of a pilot test should be very rough and tentative. It is being done only to give committee members and other campus leaders a sense of the resources needed to conduct pilot tests that answer each of the remaining questions. In many instances, pilot tests can be designed that will help the committee answer several questions at the same time.

Identifying New Skills and Knowledge. The planning committee should then identify components that require new skills, additional knowledge, and/or further experience on the part of the people who will be conducting the target academic program and then determine where these skills, knowledge, and/or experiences are to be acquired. At Seton Hill College (Pennsylvania), an annual report (Boyle, 1982, p. 3) includes the following description of the use of pilot testing to promote new faculty learning: "One of the goals of core renewal at Seton Hill is faculty renewal. Every plan for revision of the curriculum, therefore, depends upon a plan for faculty development. Four faculty members from three different disciplines participated in the pilot test. The QUE team hoped that by the end of the pilot project the participating faculty members would: (a) learn several theories of student development and apply appropriate theory to course planning and design; (b) apply student learning theory to the other courses they taught; (c) display an on-going awareness of the relationship among disciplines; (d) collaborate with other faculty members in course planning and evaluation; (e) share what they had learned with their colleagues."

While the desired learning outcomes for Seton Hill faculty are quite ambitious and extend far beyond the confines of the target academic program, they remind us of the potential impact of a successful pilot-test program and of the benefit that can be derived from many pilot tests for other academic programs at the college or university. We often forget that what a faculty member learns in planning for and pilot testing one academic program is often transferable to other programs and even to noninstructional aspects of the faculty member's professional life. A more extensive description of the Seton Hill pilot-test program is found in Case Study Nine.

CASE STUDY NINE
Seton Hill College
Greensburg, Pennsylvania

Target Academic Program: Core Curriculum
Primary Source: Boyle (1982)

Members of the planning committee at Seton Hill College faced two large tasks in September of 1981. They had previously selected revitalization of the core curriculum as the target academic program and were committed to changing a loosely structured set of distribution requirements into an outcomes-based common core curriculum. They had the responsibility of pilot testing and evaluating the first level of the core curriculum renewal project, the freshman seminars, and they had to continue to develop and design the remaining elements of the core.

The design for the pilot test actually began in January of 1981 with the recruitment of the faculty members who were to participate in it. The project that they were to lead had three distinct focal points: curriculum development, student development, and faculty development. Planning for the pilot test focused on the attainment of specific outcomes in each of these three areas, with much of the evaluation designed to determine how effective and growth producing (the fifth and sixth criteria of quality used by Project QUE) the new curriculum was in meeting stated outcomes. Less formal evaluation was used to determine campuswide perceptions regarding the attractiveness and distinctiveness (first and fourth criteria of quality) of the new core.

The freshman seminars, the first level of the three-tiered core curriculum project, introduced new students at the college to the basic skills and processes that they need to achieve a Seton Hill College degree. These seminars were interdisciplinary in content, emphasizing the reading of primary texts and the development of critical thinking. The work begun by students in the freshman seminars supported their progress through the remaining elements of the core and helped them choose a major.

Out of a freshman class of 175 students, 60 participated in the pilot test for the freshmen seminars, which ran from September 1981 to May 1982. The seminars, building on the student development theories of William Perry, Douglas Heath, Roy Heath, and Arthur Chickering, provided both "support" and "challenge." Students in the seminars lived on the same dorm floors (although not as room-mates), along with a resident assistant who was also the tutor for the class. The seminar leader served as the students' adviser until the end of the freshman year, when most students declare a major. The seminars began with experiential learning and were intended to encourage students to become aware of themselves as responsible and independent human beings.

Since faculty development was also an important feature of the pilot test, those faculty who taught in the pilot project met weekly with their colleagues in the project to share and criticize teaching methods, writing and reading assignments, evaluation techniques, and text selection. Pilot-project faculty members also attended off-campus and on-campus workshops on student development and designed and ran a week-long workshop on how to teach a freshman seminar for the new instructors in the seminar (once the pilot test was over). Much of the financial support for these faculty development features of the pilot project was provided through a grant from the National Endowment for the Humanities.

Selecting Pilot Tests to Be Attempted. The list of possible pilot tests based on identification of researchable questions is brought together with the list based on acquisition of needed skills, and priorities are established. This task is often rather difficult to accomplish, for it is hard to compare the importance of researchable questions with the importance of needed skills, knowledge, or experience. Yet some priorities need to be established. Often the two are interlinked—the researchable question concerns which skills or knowledge are required to successfully conduct a specific component. In this case, a single pilot test might be designed that will not only reveal the necessary skills or knowledge but also allow those conducting the pilot test to acquire these skills or knowledge. In other instances, the researchable questions must be answered in one pilot test before other pilot tests can be conducted for the acquisition of skills, knowledge, or experience.

Unfortunately, these comfortable resolutions are not always available. A campus leader must decide whether it is more important to obtain further information about the target academic program before developing a final design or for those conducting the program to have more experience with it before moving into full-scale implementation. Furthermore, the team must decide which researchable questions are most important and which skills, knowledge, or experiences are of greatest value.

As the committee deliberates about the importance of these various pilot-test outcomes, it may wish to revise or combine several of the potential tests so that they yield answers to several researchable questions or provide settings in which several types of skills, knowledge, or experience can be acquired. In doing this, the committee members must be careful not to overload a pilot test with too heavy an agenda. A pilot test can become so big, complex, and important that it will neither yield unambiguous answers nor be a safe place for learning and experimentation to occur but in fact become nearly the same as full-scale implementation of the program. Conflicts concerning the establishment of priorities for pilot tests should not be resolved by overinclusion or by overburdening the pilot tests.

A list of pilot tests should be drawn up by the planning committee that (1) briefly describes the rough design for each test, (2) indicates the researchable questions to be addressed by each test, and (3) indicates the priority assigned to each test. The committee should next look at its time schedule for Phase Four and its available resources in order to select one or two pilot tests that it first wants to design and implement. At Seton Hill College (Pennsylvania), the QUE team handled the problem of generating and selecting among alternative pilot-test proposals by inviting faculty members to submit proposals for pilot testing specific aspects of their target academic program (freshman seminars). Several faculty members submitted proposals in which they described how their seminars would lead to the freshman student outcomes previously identified for this program. The QUE planning committee evaluated each of these faculty proposals and selected four for inclusion in the pilot phase of the project.

At this point in Phase Four, the planning committee might wish to break into several task-force groups, each group being assigned a specific pilot test. Alternatively, people from outside the team might be brought in to help with specific pilot tests.

Certainly all people who are going to help conduct the full-scale program should be included at this point (if not already involved on the planning committee) to assist in the design and implementation of those pilot tests that directly affect their own areas of the target academic program. The committee members are now ready to move to step three (designing pilot tests) though will probably return to the list during later steps of Phase Four in order to revise it on the basis of experiences with the first pilot tests.

Step Three: Designing the Pilot Test

- *Responsibilities*
  Those who will be conducting the pilot test design the test in consultation with the planning committee and/or members of a task force assigned to oversee the test.
- *Tasks to Be Accomplished*
  1. Identify desired outcomes for the pilot test.
  2. Design an ideal pilot test.
  3. Review resources available for and constraints associated with this pilot test.
  4. Design a realistic pilot test.

Each pilot test that has been identified by the committee as being of high priority becomes a miniature target academic program when it is being designed. As in the case of the overall program design (Phase Three), the expected outcomes of the pilot test should be identified first, and then an ideal design should be formulated. An assessment of resources and constraints is then conducted, with a realistic design emerging from this assessment. While the pilot-test design process will take much less time than the overall design of a target academic program, it should at least touch on all of the steps described in Phase Three.

Identifying Desired Learning Outcomes—Student and Faculty. In the identification of desired outcomes for the pilot test, it is important to keep in mind its primary purpose as an occasion for determining the answers to researchable questions and/or the acquisition of new skills, knowledge, or experiences. While some of the outcomes should relate to student learning, others should relate to faculty learning and insights gained by those who are observing or evaluating the program.

The pressure to demonstrate that a pilot test will work— that is, will achieve certain desirable student learning outcomes— is often quite intense. While the demonstration of successful student development is often very exciting, a planning committee should be cautious about limiting their attention to these outcomes. To determine that a pilot test has been successful in achieving specific student learning outcomes tells one nothing about why this has occurred. Unless we know something about the reasons for the success of any pilot program, we rarely will be able to replicate this effect on a consistent basis. Keeping these cautionary words in mind, we offer a list of hypothetical outcomes that might be appropriate for a pilot test on the critical-thinking component of a general education program:

Student Learning Outcomes

1. Students who have completed the critical-thinking component will be able to identify and apply five principles of problem analysis when presented with three case studies.
2. Students who have completed the critical-thinking component will have applied a six-step planning process in determining their own education program over the next academic year and will have received a satisfactory evaluation from two peers and their instructor for these plans.

Researchable Question Outcomes

1. By the end of this pilot test, the planning committee will have determined whether students find this approach to critical thinking more ''stimulating'' and ''relevant'' than the critical-thinking component to which they were exposed in the ''History of Western Thought'' course they took as freshmen.
2. By the end of this pilot test, the planning committee will have determined whether the six-step planning process that they are introducing in this component is more successfully taught (in terms of student mastery of the process) by means of lecturing than by means of guided design.

Faculty Skills, Knowledge, and Experience

1. By the end of this pilot test, participating faculty will have formulated an operational definition of critical thinking that is acceptable to all members of the committee.
2. Within the first two weeks of the pilot test, faculty participants will be working effectively in a team-teaching format, as determined by members of the planning committee who are observing this teaching performance.
3. By the end of this pilot test, two of the participating faculty will have read two books on critical thinking and creative problem solving and integrated them into their teaching of critical thinking.

This list illustrates several important factors that should be kept in mind when formulating pilot-test outcomes. First, the outcomes should exemplify the basic principals of outcomes formulation that were discussed in Phase Two (step three). Second, this list of outcomes should illustrate the potential relationship between different kinds of outcomes. The second student outcome (use of the planning process for determining educational future) relates directly to the second research outcome (student assessment of the planning process). The first of these outcomes refers to the student's success in using a particular skill; the second to the best way in which to teach this skill to students. Were we successful in teaching this component (researchable question two), and did students appreciate what we taught them (researchable question one)? During a pilot test, this sort of linkage between outcomes is frequently found and is quite desirable. Third, the list should illustrate the diversity of outcomes for a pilot test. Attitudinal outcomes (researchable question one) often are more appropriate in a pilot test than in a full-scale academic program. Do participating students value what we are doing? Do members of the committee or other campus leaders like what they see about this pilot test?

    Flexibility is required in the formulation of outcomes for a pilot test. Otherwise, the pilot test will be artificially constructed. Room must also be left in the planning process for serendipity. In the pilot test, more than anywhere else in the

program planning process, the committee should be open to—
even welcome—the new and unexpected. Some of the outcomes
of a pilot test, therefore, necessarily cannot be specified beforehand. At Notre Dame College of Ohio, for instance, the pilot
test was found to be quite successful and was enthusiastically
embraced by both faculty and students. During post-test discussions, however, those conducting the test concluded that the project was too complex as an ongoing activity for the college and
hence modified their target academic program (see Case Study
Ten).

CASE STUDY TEN
Notre Dame College of Ohio
Cleveland, Ohio

Target Academic Program. Core Curriculum
Primary Source: More (1983a)

The planning committee at Notre Dame College of Ohio wanted
to pilot test a freshman seminar as part of its core curriculum revision. During the fall of 1981, the top students in the freshman class
were invited to attend a pilot seminar. They received no credit for
this seminar but could use the paper or project produced for at least
two other courses. Enough faculty and staff volunteered to teach in
the seminar that every discipline could be represented.

During the seminar, a historical perspective was supplied
through use of two introductory lectures and discussions. Five subsequent sessions focused on interdisciplinary topics (for example, ''The
Infor-sphere''). These all-inclusive topics provided opportunity for
representatives from every discipline in the college to become involved.
Thirty faculty members (about 40 percent of the total faculty), including a few persons in counseling and placement, became active
participants. The program called for presentations both from the
faculty whose special area was being handled and from students working on selected topics in the respective area. This interaction between
faculty and students was identified as one of the principal objectives
of the project and as one of its most significant outcomes.

Both faculty and student evaluations of the seminar were enthusiastic, but the consensus was that it was too complicated in its
present form to be used as a model for the rest of the core curriculum.
The form that was developed required too many faculty, and students

received no credit for the extra time and energy they put into the seminar. The modified program still used a team approach but replaced existing core courses and gave both faculty and students credit for the course.

Designing the Ideal Pilot Test. The committee (or a task force working on this specific component) is now ready to assist those who are going to implement the pilot test in designing the ideal pilot test. The design group should make use of (1) the rough design of step three, (2) the outcomes just specified, and (3) the design tools described in Phase Three (step three).

In some instances, a planning group will want to use a "temporary educational simulation" (TES) design when pilot testing components of their target academic program. A TES enables those who will be implementing a particular component to test it out with students in an environment that is safe yet conducive to new learning. In other instances, however, a committee may wish to use one of three other kinds of pilot tests: (1) a hypothetical program, (2) a closed dress rehearsal, or (3) an open ("critiqued") dress rehearsal (Bergquist and Armstrong, 1985).

A hypothetical pilot test requires that the academic program component to be tested is described in some detail and then given to some "jury" for analysis and critique. A description of the new critical-thinking component in a general education program, for instance, might be sent to potential students or to faculty at other colleges or universities who are conducting similar courses. Comments from students or faculty colleagues then can be used to modify the program design. While, in one sense, this is not a pilot test (in that the program is not being tested while actually in operation), it is a pilot test in the sense that the reactions of specific people to the design are being tested. This type of pilot test is appropriate if the component diverges significantly from traditional designs or if initial tests of the design would require significant risk to students, faculty, or the institution. The reactions of a specific population (for example, potential students) to a new program idea may be essential before designing a TES to operationally pilot test this component. Expert opinion (legal or educational) might be required before moving into untested areas. A hypothetical pilot test might ask only for evaluative responses or might ask the respondent to imagine how he or she would react to a specific set of circumstances. It might involve role playing of probable responses to a specific set of circumstances. It also might involve ratings by respondents of several possible scenarios concerning outcomes of the component being pilot tested.

The closed dress rehearsal is another kind of pilot test. It is employed when skills need to be polished or a bit more experience is needed but no researchable question has been posed and no major new learning is required. When a program component requires a "performance" (for example, joint teaching, debate, or interview), it may be valuable for the presenters to try it out once or twice without benefit of an audience (students) or even evaluators (other than themselves and others involved in the program). A closed dress rehearsal enables faculty to take risks without repercussion, to try out several alternative courses of action, and to determine whether the pieces fit together as they were originally envisioned. In planning for this type of pilot test, a planning committee should be sensitive to the possible loss of spontaneity and motivation if an instructional performance or team project is overrehearsed. Debates, role plays, and interviews, for instance, often lose some of their spark if rehearsed ahead of time.

The open ("critiqued") dress rehearsal is a final form of pilot test. This form blends the first two and moves the committee toward a TES. A program component is presented before an audience (for example, colleagues, potential students, experts) and is subjected to a critique by this audience. The audience might actually be physically present while the component is being presented, or the presentation might be audiotaped or (preferably) videotaped and played at a later point to members of the audience. A live presentation will convey more of the "spirit" of the program. A videotape of the presentation, however, can be played at a time that is convenient for those offering a critique (particularly important if outside experts are to review the presentation) and can be replayed many times by those doing the review (as well as those making the presentation). Performance anxiety is often reduced as well if the audience is not "live."

This type of pilot test provides faculty with feedback (as does the hypothetical program) as well as an opportunity to gain further experience in trying out a new component. As in the case of the hypothetical program, the "critiqued" dress rehearsal is appropriate when the component to be tested is controversial or potentially detrimental in terms of student learning or institutional reputation or, as with the closed dress rehearsal, when the component involves complex relationships between people, pieces of equipment, and so on. King's College (New York) was faced with the latter situation when developing its new career development program. Complex interinstitutional relationships had to be negotiated in order to set up student internships. The planning committee for this Project QUE college decided to use an "open dress rehearsal" in order to work through these issues. At Huntington College (Indiana), three complex components required the use of "critiqued" dress rehearsals. One of these was a "cocurricular" component of the Huntington target academic program, while the other two involved specific courses that were being pilot tested (see Case Study Eleven).

CASE STUDY ELEVEN
Huntington College
Huntington, Indiana

Target Academic Program: Business and Economics Curriculum
Primary Source: Hale (1983)

The first pilot test conducted by the planning committee at Huntington College, in the spring of 1982, concerned the formation of a student business organization. Project QUE paid the dues of approximately thirty members and funded an organizational pizza party. The students were asked to participate and determine whether the organization was worthwhile for Huntington's cocurricular component of the target academic program. This pilot test represents a "critiqued dress rehearsal" mode of pilot testing.

The evaluation of the effectiveness of the business organization was done through a student attitude survey, taken informally by the sponsor after the students had participated in both state and national conventions of Phi Beta Lambda (a national business fraternity). The results were overwhelmingly positive. The organization is now a full-fledged chapter of this fraternity and has its own student office on campus.

The second pilot test, conducted in the fall of 1982, tested a new team-taught course entitled "Introduction to Business." The course was evaluated by the students through a survey instrument and by the Project QUE committee on the basis of the instructor's own comments. The results from these evaluations led to the decision to limit this course to first-time freshman students (excluding non-majors and upper-class students). The student evaluation also indicated that several of the topics were not appropriate for the introductory level of the course. The course was revised in response to this information, while credit for it was reduced from four semester hours to three because of the reduced number of topics being presented.

A third pilot test was conducted during the spring of 1983. A new course being designed by the mathematics department for the business program ("Mathematics for the Managerial and Social Sciences") was taught to a cross section of business students. This course was also revised in response to student evaluations, as well as comments made by the business faculty and the faculty teaching the course.

Pilot testing of particularly complex or controversial components might be sequenced. First, a hypothetical description of the component would be written, circulated, and criticized. Faculty would then try out the component in a closed dress rehearsal, taking into account the critiques that were received regarding the hypothetical program. An open dress rehearsal would be offered, so that those who criticized the hypothetical program could see the component in operation. Once again, their critiques would be solicited and used to further modify and improve the design of this component.

At this point, the committee is ready to pilot test the component with students in a temporary educational simulation. Following this TES (and maybe one or two more TESs on this component), the planning committee is ready for full-scale implementation. Obviously, this four- or five-step pilot-test sequence should be used sparingly. This level of caution and care is required for only the most difficult components.

Reviewing Available Resources. With the design of an ideal pilot test, the group planning this test should at least briefly review the resources that are available and consider constraints on the test before preparing a more realistic design. The suggestions made with regard to Phase Three about the types of information to collect and modes of analysis to use are relevant in this phase as well, though much less time should be devoted to the collection and analysis of information in planning for a pilot test.

If nothing else, the planning group should pause after the design of an ideal pilot test to determine whether (1) the people who will run this pilot test actually have time to fully participate in it, (2) the people who are to observe, assess, and evaluate the pilot test have time to successfully complete this task, and (3) sufficient money, materials, equipment (especially recording equipment), and space are available to run the pilot test with minimal administrative distraction. Typically, a pilot test is an add-on to an already full schedule of activities. Faculty are trying to keep up with their current courses and have little time to plan for new ones. Even less time is available to observe, assess, or evaluate the work of another faculty member. Furthermore, because the pilot test is a temporary activity that usually does not readily fit into any bureaucratic "niche," there are often administrative entanglements that drain time and energy away from the pilot test itself. These factors must be taken into consideration and overcome if the pilot test is to be successful.

Designing a Realistic Pilot Test. The planning group should now be ready to realistically design the pilot test, taking into account these constraints and limitations in resources. In some instances, the planning committee might wish to invite in colleagues to review the ideal design. At St. Mary's Dominican College (Louisiana), for instance, each of three pilot tests was reviewed by a "design review panel" composed of faculty members, students, staff, and alumni.

In designing a realistic program and possibly conferring with other constituencies on campus, the planning group should always keep in mind that this is a pilot test and not the real thing. Practical matters must be kept in mind; however, the pilot test should not be stifled by pragmatism—there is no better place to be idealistic and a bit daring than in a pilot test. Care also must be taken not to overplan the pilot test; otherwise, the serendipity will escape and a rare opportunity will be lost for significant new learning to occur among faculty, students, and other participants.

Step Four: Initiating the Pilot Test

- *Responsibilities*
  Faculty, academic administrators, and others who will be involved in the full-scale implementation of the component being pilot tested conduct the test in consultation with the committee or members of a task force assigned to oversee this pilot test.
- *Task to Be Accomplished*
  Dependent on the purpose and design of the pilot test.

Providing Time for Reflection. Though implementation of strategies will vary greatly according to the purpose and design of the pilot test, several factors should be kept in mind. First, sufficient time should be set aside for talking about the pilot test after it is completed. Often pilot tests are of only moderate value because the participants and observers do not take sufficient time to analyze and discuss the results. At least one hour of post-test discussion should accompany every five hours of pilot testing. Furthermore, post-test discussions should be scheduled both immediately after the pilot test and at a later point (usually at least one week after its conclusion) so that both short-term and longer-term perspectives are available. Unless the pilot test is very short or not easily interrupted, discussion should also take place at one or more points while it is in progress.

Focusing on Faculty Learning Outcomes. A second factor to keep in mind is the importance of nonstudent learning outcomes in a pilot test. Particularly in the implementation of a TES, faculty are inclined to forget that this is a pilot test and that their own learning is just as important as that of the participating students. They are inclined to retreat to established patterns of behavior and refer to old skills, knowledge, and experiences in order to be certain that the students are receiving a satisfactory education. While this concern is commendable, faculty who are participating in pilot tests sometimes need to be reminded about the importance of other outcomes and reassured that in most instances students learn as much from educational experiences in which the learning of faculty is deemed to be important as they do in normal student-oriented educational settings.

Preparing People for the Experience. Third, in the implementation of a pilot test, participants, observers, and interested bystanders need to be prepared for a level of emotional intensity that rarely is present in usual educational activities. If a pilot test is being used to explore new areas, to answer difficult questions, or to provide opportunities for faculty and others to acquire new skills, knowledge, and/or experience, then one can expect this pilot test to trigger personal, interpersonal, and organizational stress.

In the pilot-test context, faculty will often re-examine their own values and assumptions about education, life, and career plans and images of themselves as lecturers, advisers, colleagues, innovators, or scholars (Bergquist, Lounibos, and Langfitt, 1980). Faculty and students often will begin to explore new student-faculty, faculty-faculty, and student-student relationships and new modes of decision making, problem solving, conflict management, and leadership in the unique interpersonal and organizational setting of the pilot test (see also Case Study Ten). If participants and observers of a pilot test are aware that this stress can occur and that personal, interpersonal, and organizational discomfort may be essential for significant learning to occur, then they are less likely to react precipitously when the stress becomes apparent. They can even plan for its occurrence by bringing in an external or, preferably, an on-campus resource person with past experience in pilot tests. This person can assist with the post-test discussion as well as be available during the pilot test for individual, small-group, or total-group consultation.

Defining a Proper Role for Assessment. Fourth, while assessment of the pilot test must be given adequate attention, it should not dominate the pilot test. Neither students nor faculty should feel like guinea pigs who are constantly being monitored, tested, or manipulated by some outside agency. For the assessment of a pilot test to be beneficial, it must be carefully planned and executed in full consultation with those conducting it. We turn now to this planning step.

Step Five: Assessing the Pilot Test

- *Responsibilities*
  An assessment team, selected by the planning committee and participants in the pilot test, designs and conducts program assessment in conjunction with the committee and pilot-test participants.
- *Tasks to Be Accomplished*
  1. Select the people who will conduct the assessment.
  2. Determine the program dimensions, activities, and outcomes that will be assessed in the pilot test.
  3. Determine strategies and select tools for the assessment of the pilot test.
  4. Implement the assessment procedure.
  5. Analyze and synthesize the information collected during the program assessment and prepare oral and written reports on this analysis and synthesis.
  6. Report findings to the committee and participants in the pilot test.

This fifth step, planning and implementing the assessment of the pilot test, should actually parallel rather than follow the previous four steps. Planning for the assessment should begin during step two, when priorities are being established for each possible pilot test. When constraints are being considered during step two, the planning committee should at least briefly review the feasibility of assessing each possible pilot test. If a pilot test cannot be assessed rather easily, then the committee should ask whether it should be conducted at all. This is especially the case if the pilot test is to address a researchable question.

Selecting the Assessors. Planning for pilot-test assessment should be integral to the process of designing the pilot test during step three. Once the pilot tests have been identified (step two), an assessment team should be selected. Preferably, this team should include someone who knows something about program evaluation, as well as someone who knows something about the area in which the pilot test is being conducted but who is not directly associated with the target academic program being assessed. The team might also include a student, other faculty members, an alumnus, or even a trustee. It need not be very large (two people are often sufficient) and will vary widely in composition according to the nature of the pilot test.

At Marian College (Indiana), the planning committee appointed an evaluation team to monitor its pilot-test course (global studies) that consisted of a faculty member from the psychology department, a member of the board of trustees at the college (and a dean at a nearby public university), and the college librarian (who was auditing the pilot-test course). This team prepared a report at the end of the pilot project that complemented the planning committee's use of performance tests to determine whether the desired student learning outcomes were being achieved.

In several cases, Project QUE committees decided to make use of only one person as the assessment team. Typically, as in the case of Regis College (Massachusetts), this person was an external evaluator or consultant with specific expertise in the area being pilot tested. The specific assessments that were done by this consultant were often complemented by additional evaluations by the planning committee itself. At Regis College, for instance, the committee collected evaluations from students and alumni who had participated in their pilot career-awareness program.

Regardless of the assessment team composition, it is essential that this team provide the pilot test with a knowledgeable and critical perspective. It should not simply rubber stamp the decisions of those conducting the pilot test. Someone on the assessment team should represent the interests and concerns of the planning committee. Someone else, if possible, should represent other relevant interests on campus—though the primary task is not to make the target academic program more responsive to these particular interests but to help the planning committee answer its researchable questions.

Determining Aspects of the Pilot Test to Be Assessed. The assessment team should determine the program dimensions, activities, and outcomes that are to be assessed in conjunction with the planning committee and those planning the pilot test during step three. Following are several of the questions that might be addressed with reference to program dimensions: (1) To what extent should the assessment focus on the results or outcomes of the pilot test and to what extent on the processes whereby these results or outcomes are or are not achieved? (2) To what extent should the assessment focus on the learning of students, faculty, and other participants in the pilot test? (3) To what extent should the assessment specifically focus on the activities of the pilot test (in isolation), and to what extent should it consider the pilot test within its educational setting? The answers to these three questions will depend on the reasons for conducting the pilot test and the type of pilot test that is selected. Researchable questions concerning student learning outcomes will yield a different type of evaluation than researchable questions concerning the cause of certain program difficulties.

Questions that should be addressed regarding program activities are: (1) Which activities appear to be critical to the achievement of specific desired outcomes of the pilot test? (2) Which activities will probably reflect most accurately the overall climate and level of success of the pilot test? (3) Which activities can be most readily observed without distracting from the learning of students, faculty, and other participants in the pilot test? A set of activities usually are selected that balance the assessment of specific program outcomes with the assessment of overall program success. If observing an activity would be distracting to those participating in the pilot test, then observation should be avoided. If the activity must be observed, then the participants' reaction to this observation must itself become part of the analysis. Sometimes, important activities should be audio- or videotaped rather than directly observed. The assessment team must realize, however, that the taping of the activity will itself have an impact—sometimes even greater than that of direct observation.

Several questions must be addressed concerning the pilot-test outcomes to be assessed: (1) How important is the assessment of formally defined outcomes of the pilot test relative to outcomes that are unanticipated (emerging during the course of the pilot test)? (2) How important is the assessment of the extent to which an outcome is achieved relative to the assessment of the causes for the relative success or failure of the outcome? (3) Should there be quantitative evidence for the achievement of an outcome, or will qualitative evidence be acceptable or even preferable.

Determining Strategies and Methods of Assessment. The answers to the preceding and related questions concerning program dimensions, activities, and outcomes serve as a basis for determining the assessment strategies and tools to be employed (Bergquist and Armstrong, 1985). In general, pilot tests conducted to answer researchable questions require more extensive evaluation. Pilot tests conducted for the acquisition of skills, knowledge, or experience usually require less evaluation. A TES will usually require more extensive evaluation than will other kinds of pilot tests. The closed dress rehearsal usually requires the least amount of formal evaluation.

Pilot tests that address questions concerning the effectiveness of particular techniques or designs will emphasize outcome determination evaluation, often making use of a pre–post experimental or quasi-experimental assessment design (Campbell and Stanley, 1966). Extensive program description and documentation are important if a faculty member is trying to gain more experience in conducting a component of the academic program and wishes to review aspects of this experience even after the pilot test is completed, or if the pilot test is being used to ''sell'' the complete target academic program to one or more constituencies.

Selecting Assessment Tools. A variety of tools can be used for the assessment of a pilot test, some of them yielding qualitative evidence and others quantitative (Pilon and Bergquist, 1979; Bergquist and Armstrong, 1985). When pre–post measures are to be taken, performance tests and/or questionnaires may be appropriate. The College of Notre Dame (Maryland) assessed the student learning outcome results from its pilot tests through use of the writing and speaking components of the Comprehensive Outcome Measures Program (COMP) tests that have been developed by the American College Testing (ACT) organization. Making use of different versions of COMP-ACT in pre- and post-testing of treatment and control groups, the College of Notre Dame's planning committee found twice as much improvement in writing drills in the pilot-test courses than in the control-group courses and a smaller but statistically significant gain in speaking skills. Performance tests were also used to assess the effectiveness of a pilot test at the College of Mount St. Vincent (New York). Unlike the planning committee at the College of Notre Dame, those conducting the assessment at the College of Mount St. Vincent devised their own performance tests (see Case Study Twelve).

CASE STUDY TWELVE
College of Mount St. Vincent
Riverdale, New York

Target Academic Program: International Economics/Business
Primary Source: Higgins (1982)

As part of its Project QUE pilot test, the College of Mount St. Vincent planning committee worked on the design of pre- and post–pilot-test procedures and the assessment of outcomes of a course in international political economy. The head of this committee reported that:

the students in the International Political Economics course included juniors and sophomores, all of whom had completed a course within two years in macro- or microeconomics. Most had declared their intention of specializing in International Business. Beyond these two constants, their backgrounds in political science, sociology, and foreign civilization courses were varied.

The control group was chosen to match the academic level and size of the primary group; none of these students, however, had indicated any interest in International Business. Some had had the introductory courses in economics and sociology.

A closed-ended written test was designed, with the collaboration of all three International Political Economy faculty. The test was kept simple rather than complex in design, to avoid the ambiguity that a more ambitious pattern might yield. With this end in mind a psychometrician from the College faculty was called upon to examine the first draft.

The course had been developed in the hope that it would broaden student opinion and understanding of other cultures. The psychologist consulted pointed out the difficulty of measuring attitudinal changes and felt that the material initially presented for testing would yield data only on the acquisition of knowledge. Conferences between faculty and the consultant resulted in a revamped testing instrument, still not entirely satisfactory for measurement of attitudinal change, but at least an improvement—and a compromise.

The test finally agreed upon consisted of two sections asking for the "best" answer—yes or no—to each question, the consultant's feeling being that there is no such thing as a "true" true-false question. The third component—that submitted by the sociologist—was a multiple-choice test. Not surprisingly, this segment seemed most likely to measure attitude.

The tests were administered to the International Political Economy class and to the control group at the same time, the pre-test near the beginning of the course and the post-test at the end of the Spring term.

The control group was chosen from an English class taught by a member of the QUE planning team. The test was conducted during class—in order to simulate as closely as possible the conditions in the IPE class [p. 2].

The international political economy class achieved significantly greater gains with regard to the outcomes that were tested than did the control group, thus giving the teaching team important encouragement for implementation of the course as a regular offering. Through collaboration with social science colleagues, members of the planning committee also learned something about outcomes test design that would be of use to them in the future.

In-process assessment can take place through use of interviews, observations, participant observations, and/or obtrusive (reactive) measures, while postevent assessment can take place by means of questionnaires, retrospective interviews, document review, unobtrusive measures, critical-incident checklists, and/or the introduction of information about other programs. At Columbia Union College (Maryland), where a cooperative education program was being pilot tested with twelve students, the accomplishment of learning outcomes and the strengths and weaknesses of program components and procedures were assessed through use of questionnaires given to students, staff supervisors, department chairs, and cooperating agency personnel.

A desired institutional outcome at Huntingdon College (Alabama) was improved retention of superior-ability students through establishment of an honors program. The best assessment of the potential future effectiveness of this program was through measurement of the retention of the sixteen freshman students in the pilot group. Fifteen of those students returned the next fall, a clearly superior retention rate when compared to that for similar students not participating in the program or attending the college in previous years.

At King's College (New York) (Gustafson, 1982, p. 3), "reviewing the methods to assess both program effectiveness and student learning outcomes that were suggested in the Project [QUE] Work Manual was worthwhile. Lack of time and 'people' resources were important constraints that led us ultimately to use a questionnaire which directed its attention to such important items as the effect of the practicum on student attitudes about: (a) academic courses of study, (b) the nature of work, (c) professional work performance standards, (d) professional career plans, (e) personal Christian faith and values, (f) adequacy of communication skills, (g) adequacy of analytical skills. This questionnaire also sought to assess the value of each of the following as aids in achieving the goals of the student's learning contract: (a) the role of the field supervisor, (b) the work experience, (c) the faculty advisor, (d) the writing of an introspective journal.''

Implementing the Assessment and Analyzing Results. Appropriate strategies and tools should be selected by the assessment team in close cooperation with the planning committee and those conducting the pilot test. When implementing the assessment, members of the team should continue to work closely with these constituencies to be sure that the right type of information is being collected and that the assessment procedure itself is not disrupting the pilot test more than anticipated. The assessment team should report findings as soon as possible. Early reports can help those conducting the pilot test to modify the design of the test while there still is time to observe the effects of this modification. When all feedback is held to the end of the pilot test, another pilot test often is required before the effects of the modification can be noted. In many instances, of course, results and observations cannot be reported until the pilot test is completed, because the effects will not be known until that time or because an early report will bias the results obtained, making the test invalid for outcome-determination purposes.

Reporting Assessment Results. The assessment team should first present its results orally to the planning committee and those conducting the pilot test, then prepare a written report that provides a more detailed analysis. An adequate period of time for discussion, analysis, and synthesis by members of the assessment team should always precede data feedback. With the press of time that is often associated with a pilot test, assessment teams are likely to spend too little time comparing notes and distilling findings. As a result, planning committee members and those conducting the pilot test are often overwhelmed or confused by the extensive and contradictory data that are presented.

Major themes should be identified by the team. Data that are specifically responsive to the concerns and questions identified by the planning committee and pilot-test leaders should be given priority. The assessment team should avoid the temptation of giving too much attention to issues that it thinks important but that are not deemed important by the planning committee. Members of the team (and the planning committee), however, should remain open to the exploration of serendipitous outcomes and lessons that were not anticipated by either the planning committee or the assessment team.

While those conducting the pilot test and members of the planning committee will add their own experiences and evaluations to those of the assessment team, the role of this latter group is critical if those responsible for the target academic program and the pilot test are to receive a relatively unbiased and fresh perspective on the often complex and controversial component of an academic program that is being pilot tested.

Step Six: Reviewing and Revising
Components of the Target Academic Program

- *Responsibilities*
  Faculty, academic administrators, and others who will be involved in the full-scale implementation of the component that was pilot tested, together with members of the planning committee (or members of a task force assigned to this component), review the pilot-test results and determine what changes, if any, are needed in the program design.
- *Tasks to Be Accomplished*
  1. Discuss the assessment team's oral and written reports in conjunction with the personal experiences of those participating in the pilot test.
  2. Determine the answers to researchable questions and/or review skills, knowledge, and experiences acquired during the pilot test. Determine the extent to which researchable questions have been answered and acquisition outcomes identified during step three have been achieved.
  3. Compare student learning outcomes obtained from the pilot test with the expected student learning outcomes identified during step three.
  4. Identify forces within or operating on the pilot test that facilitate or block accomplishment of the intended student learning outcomes and that facilitate or reduce impact of unanticipated (both positive and negative) student learning outcomes of the pilot test.

5. Estimate the extent to which the pilot test artificially influenced the answers obtained (researchable questions), skills, knowledge, and experiences acquired, and/or forces observed in association with each student learning outcome.

6. Recommend redesign of this component of the target academic program if necessary, making use of answers to the researchable questions, skills, knowledge, and experiences acquired, and force-field analysis.

7. Decide whether further pilot tests of this component should be conducted. If so, return to step three. If another component is to be pilot tested, return to the end of step two. If all pilot testing has been completed, move on to step seven.

Reviewing Assessment Results. Upon completion of the pilot test and the reports of the assessment team, the pilot-test leaders and committee (or task force) are ready to review results from the pilot test and determine what changes, if any, should be made in this component of the academic program. Those conducting the pilot test and planning committee members should first consider their own experience with the pilot test—either as participants or as observers—in relationship to the assessment team's report. If there are any significant discrepancies, the assessment team should be invited back for further discussion and even further data collection if necessary and feasible.

Discussing Pilot-Test Findings. Initially, the review group may wish to determine the answers to any questions that were posed during step five and consider revisions in this program component. The group should next review acquired skills, knowledge, and experiences to help the planning committee to determine whether more pilot tests of this component are needed and whether any revisions in the design are required because of the inability of those conducting the pilot test to master certain skills or acquire certain knowledge relevant to this component. Following this, the review group should turn to student learning outcomes that were identified during step three: (1) Which of the original student learning outcomes have been achieved in this pilot test? (2) Which of the original student learning outcomes have not been achieved in this pilot test? Why not? (3) If step three were to be repeated, would the list of desired student learning outcomes change given the results of this pilot test? Why? In addition, the review group should identify any unanticipated yet significant outcomes of the pilot test: (1) Were the unanticipated outcomes positive or negative with reference to the desired student learning outcomes of this component? (2) Can these outcomes be purposefully achieved or avoided in the future?

Conducting Force-Field Analysis. Making use of the information obtained from the researchable questions, the skills, knowledge, and experience acquired, and the assessment of anticipated and unanticipated student learning outcomes, the review group is prepared to conduct a force-field analysis:

Positive Forces

1. For each of the major student learning outcomes of the pilot test, which were the forces (events, people, money, time, machines, and so on) operating within or from outside the pilot test that facilitated its accomplishment?
2. How strong were each of these forces with specific reference to this outcome?
3. To what extent are these forces susceptible to change?
4. How confident and clear are members of the review group about the facilitating effect, strength, and susceptibility to change of each force, with specific reference to each outcome?

Negative Forces

1. For each of the major student learning outcomes of the pilot test, what were the internal and external forces that seemed to block its accomplishment?
2. How strong was each of these forces with specific reference to this outcome?
3. To what extent is each of these forces resistant to change?
4. How confident and clear are members of the review group about the blocking effect, strength, and ability to resist change of each force, with specific reference to each outcome?

Estimating Differences Between the Pilot Test and the Full-Scale Program. After the analysis is completed, the review group should attempt to estimate the extent to which each of the forces that have been identified is unique to this particular pilot test or probably would be present if this component, as currently designed, were to be implemented as part of a full-scale academic program. Similarly, the review group should estimate the extent to which answers to the researchable questions might have been biased by the experimental condition (pilot test) and the extent to which the skills, knowledge, and experiences acquired during the pilot test might be inappropriate when applied during the full-scale implementation of the program. One can only speculate about these differences at this point; determining whether the conditions of the pilot test were truly representative must await full-scale implementation.

When estimating the potential differences between the pilot test and the "real world," it is particularly important to keep in mind the so-called "Hawthorne effect" that operates during many pilot tests: students, faculty, observers, and others know that this is an experiment or attempted innovation and will thus often give an extra effort to make it work—or will at least be more tolerant of failure and more inclined to give other people the benefit of the doubt. On the more negative side, a pilot test, as a temporary system, will often be taken less seriously than a more permanent program and will be added on to other existing responsibilities and program activities. These "artificial" elements must be factored out or at least taken into account before the planning committee considers possible changes in the design of this program component.

Refining the Design. At this point in the pilot-testing process, the review group's work is completed, for recommendations concerning revision of the design should be made by the planning committee and included with recommendations about other components in the final overall program review process of step seven. These recommendations are often difficult to make. Members of the committee and, in particular, participants in the pilot test often feel a great deal of ownership for the present design of a program component. Unfortunately, the effort expended in designing and implementing a pilot test will sometimes further reinforce this sense of ownership and resistance to change. Yet the pilot test was meant to be experimental and to facilitate the process of design review and revision.

Changes in the design should build on answers to researchable questions that have been posed and should make effective use of the skills, knowledge, and experiences that have been acquired. The new design should reinforce facilitating forces that are strong but potentially subject to change, build on facilitating forces that are strong and enduring, reduce strong but changeable forces that are blocking, and avoid those blocking forces that are strong and resistant to change. Planning committee members and those conducting the pilot test may also wish to recommend more general changes in the overall program design, having identified forces that were external to the pilot-test component. If the assessment team has conducted an evaluation that examines the pilot test in a broad context, the review group might be particularly interested in making several general recommendations regarding the program.

A frequent benefit of the pilot testing done by many Project QUE colleges concerned the sequencing of course content. Dominican College of Blauvelt (New York), for instance, pilot tested three new courses for a business administration program in information systems management. As a result of the pilot test, the planning committee revised the sequence in which the three courses would be taken. In particular, new attention was given to the background possessed by a large number of transfer students entering the program. Illinois Benedictine College's pilot test of its scholars program incorporated not only program components, curricular content, and teaching methods but also recruiting, interviewing, and selection procedures. Ten selected students participated in the pilot program, which assisted the college's planning committee in revising the recruiting process and selection methods, increasing the grade-point-average equivalent, and refining the mentoring system.

Determining Whether Further Pilot Testing Is Needed. The task of reviewing the component completed, the planning committee should now determine whether any more pilot tests need to be conducted for this component: (1) Have all the researchable questions been answered satisfactorily? (2) Have the needed skills, knowledge, and experience been acquired? (3) Do those conducting this component feel comfortable about moving on to its full-scale implementation? (4) Do the proposed design modifications require more testing? If more pilot testing is desired, then the planning committee (or task force) and participants in this program component should return to step three in order to reformulate desired outcomes for the pilot test and design a new pilot test to achieve these outcomes. If no further work is required on this component, then the committee should either turn to another component (end of step two) or move on to step seven (overall review of the program design).

Several Project QUE colleges found that they had to rerun pilot tests as a result of what was learned from the first pilot test. Roberts Wesleyan's (New York) report, for instance, describes the following pilot-test activities (Ogden, 1983, p. 3): "A set of student outcomes for listening, reading, speaking, thinking and writing was developed and an integrated approach to teaching speech and writing was pilot-tested in the spring of 1982. However, it was discovered that the student sample was quite atypical in many ways; for this reason the pilot test was repeated in the fall of 1982 with a more representative sample of students."

Multiple pilot testing was also required at Olivet College (Michigan). The planning committee at Olivet piloted a freshman and sophomore core program as well as thirteen individual courses during the fall of 1981. Twenty-five faculty members (over 50 percent of the entire faculty) were involved in this pilot testing. They found that they learned much during these pilot tests and during several workshops that they attended, and so a second series of pilot tests was conducted during the spring semester. These pilot tests were "more tightly structured during the second semester, 1981–82, and a plan for generating faculty feedback was developed. The [planning] committee decided that Phase IV should be an 'advanced pilot' phase and that a systematic evaluation plan should be worked out for this phase" (Epstein, 1983, p. 3). Thus, the planning committee at Olivet College built not only upon its pilot-test experiences but also upon its experiences in evaluating the pilot test, by offering a sequence of three different groups of pilot tests for its core curriculum revision.

Step Seven: Reviewing the Overall Target Academic Program in Light of Pilot-Test Results

- *Responsibilities*
  The planning committee reviews all pilot-test results and makes changes in the overall program design.
- *Tasks to Be Accomplished*
  1. Assemble and review all assessment reports, recommended changes in program components, and recommendations for changes in the overall design.
  2. Determine whether any changes need to be made in the overall target academic program design.
  3. Determine whether any additional information needs to be collected with reference to these changes in the design (requiring a return to step two for planning of more pilot tests).
  4. Prepare the final design of the target academic program for full-scale implementation.

Reviewing All Results from Pilot Testing. At the point when all of the pilot tests have been completed, the planning committee is approaching the end of Phase Four. Each college or university will have reached this point in its own unique way. Some colleges and universities will have initiated many pilot tests; others will have conducted only one. Whenever the planning committee is ready to move toward full-scale implementation of the target academic program, there is one final planning step that should be taken: the planning committee should review the pilot-test results in order to determine whether any of the recommended changes that emerged from step six should be initiated in the design of the target program.

Deciding on Design Changes. In many instances, changes in the overall design will be made on an ongoing basis, as pilot-test results come in to the planning committee for discussion and review. In other instances, the planning committee will collect all of the recommendations and refrain from making any final decisions until all of the pilot tests have been completed. Regardless of the method used, one final session concerning the program should be held. At this session, one important question should be addressed: Are there any overall patterns or themes in the pilot tests that have not yet been addressed? By looking very hard at the trees (components), have we failed to see problems in the overall academic forest of this program?

Identifying Questions for Future Study. When this final review takes place, and if additional changes are made in the design, the planning committee may find that several additional questions emerge and that additional information is needed. In most cases, this can be collected in a short period of time and need not hold up full-scale implementation. In other cases, these questions can be answered soon after the program is being fully implemented.

At Marian College (Indiana), considerable concern was voiced after a pilot test was conducted on their target global studies program regarding the textbook that was used for the course. During the pilot test, the students apparently experienced considerable difficulties with the assigned text. The text was subsequently changed when the course was implemented during Phase Five. Yet questions remained regarding the reasons for the students' difficulties during the pilot test. Following the first full-scale implementation of the global studies course, the Marian College teaching team concluded that the original textbook was satisfactory—for the new textbook proved to be even more difficult for students—and that the difficulties the students had with the original text could be resolved by more adequate explanations and discussions of the text material by the teaching team. Thus, as was the case with many other QUE projects, several important questions remained after the pilot test that could be addressed during Phase Five.

A planning committee should be particularly careful at this point in the planning process to avoid stalling tactics introduced by those members who are least inclined to take a risk. These tactics may take the form of a continuing and unreasonable concern about the collection of more data or implementation of additional, unnecessary pilot tests. At some point, the target academic program must be fully implemented. Additional information can and should be collected while the program is being implemented. Every program should be accompanied by an effective formative evaluation process that addresses the continuing concerns of committee members. The time to move from reflection to action has come, however, and the target academic program is ready to be launched. The planning committee should now begin planning for the fifth and final phase: implementation, evaluation, and dissemination.

The Use of Pilot Tests: Concluding Thoughts

If there was any part of Project QUE that we were concerned about, it was participants' willingness to adopt pilot testing. However, as the colleges reached Phase Four of the project, they became very conscientious about the pilot-testing process. In fact, as noted above, several colleges decided to increase the knowledge and skills needed to implement their target academic program through a second round of pilot testing prior to full-scale implementation.

In addition to being a step in a process, pilot testing encompasses an attitude toward learning and experimentation. It is a deliberate attempt to develop and verify as much quality in a program as possible before actually engaging large numbers of students in it. This attitude was internalized by many Project QUE faculty. Evidence accumulated that pilot testing was being applied to the development of other campus programs and to day-to-day teaching and learning activities both inside and outside the target academic program.

Temporary educational simulations (TESs) were not often used during Project QUE. While a number of colleges used variations of the "course-embedded" TES, most pilot testing could best be described as "small-scale" implementation of "closed dress rehearsal." Such an approach was certainly within the spirit of the pilot-testing concept and provides other colleges and universities with a practical model of program planning and testing.

One additional central question must be asked about pilot testing: does it really make a difference? It was clearly shown in many Project QUE colleges that careful pilot testing and evaluation of pilot tests often made a difference with reference to future plans for the target academic program. In many cases, the target academic program was significantly changed as a result of pilot-test results. Trinity College (Vermont), for instance, shifted the emphases in several of its freshman seminars as a result of pilot-test feedback (see Case Study Thirteen). Even more substantial change occurred at Marymount Manhattan College (New York). Marymount Manhattan pilot tested two different methods of providing training to faculty in computer instruction, one in the fall, in which faculty attended a regularly scheduled course over an eight-week period, and one in January, which was an intensive one-week course. Evaluations by faculty indicated that a one-week course was more fruitful in terms of time demands, and the college chose the one-week model. The planning committee also determined from its pilot-test results that a one-credit course in BASIC computer language was insufficient for its students and so replaced it with a three-credit course.

CASE STUDY THIRTEEN
Trinity College
Burlington, Vermont

Target Academic Program: Freshman Seminar
Primary Source: Rodd (1983)

In the winter of 1982–83, the faculty at Trinity College were given the objectives and guidelines for the freshman seminars and invited to submit course proposals for pilot seminars. An effort was made to recruit faculty members known as "good for freshmen"—experienced and enthusiastic about teaching and advising. Three proposals were accepted, each appearing likely to be personally relevant to young women entering a new cultural setting.

The first three seminars were offered on a pilot basis to forty-three students during the fall of 1982. A randomly chosen subset of incoming traditional-aged students were sent invitations to participate until forty-five acceptances were received. Thirty-three (73 percent) were assigned to their first choice of the three seminars and the remaining students to their second choice.

Evaluation of the pilot seminars was intended to answer three broad questions: (1) Have we done in the seminars what we said we would? (2) How did it go? What did participants identify as the strengths, weaknesses, achievements, and problems of the seminars? and (3) What differences have the seminars made in the participating students, in comparison with their classmates?

With regard to the first of these questions, the seminar instructors met regularly with the project coordinator regarding assignments, activities, and teaching techniques. A midsemester evaluation interview was conducted by the project coordinator with the students in each seminar (in the instructor's absence). This interview was used to confirm the information provided by the instructors. Some differences were found among the seminars. One was characterized as being particularly warm and informal, with greater attention being given to students' out-of-class adjustment to college and less to course content; the other two instructors, by contrast, emphasized course content and structured class time more explicitly. The seminars also varied in the degree of formality of the processes used for students' self-assessment and contracting for personal learning.

The question of overall effectiveness of the seminars was addressed by asking both students and instructors to assess the strengths and weaknesses of the seminar program in comparison to other courses and other academic advisers. The information from students included the midterm course evaluation described above; an open-ended questionnaire that seminar students completed about their first semester of college; a paper-and-pencil evaluation of academic advising completed by both seminar and nonseminar students; and a conventional end-of-semester course evaluation, which was compared with evaluations of other courses in which a large proportion of students were traditional-aged freshmen. The information from instructors included a rating of how well course objectives had been met and a wealth of information provided informally in group meetings and in one-to-one conversations with the project coordinator.

The pilot-test evaluation of the target academic program (competency-based education) at Rust College (Mississippi) led not to the addition of credits for a course but rather to reduction in the size of the college's curriculum. The planning committee at Rust (McKinney, 1983, p. 2) reported that:

> before the introduction of the competency-based approach to instruction in Chemistry . . . the Chemistry faculty recommended the addition of two new courses to the curriculum to make sure Chemistry students would be adequately prepared. The process of program review analysis coupled with the preparation of detailed learning packages for the existing Chemistry courses led the faculty to a rather startling discovery. Some of the faculty using the conventional approach to instruction discovered that the old approach was proving counterproductive because of monotonous and unnecessary repetition of content in course sequences which had the effect of killing the interest of students who desired to learn more new things than to be bored to death by the repetition of things they already know. In addition, the team effort engendered by this pilot project in Chemistry with its emphasis on instructional design and proper sequencing of courses made it clear to faculty and students that the competency-based approach to instruction strengthened the program by eliminating useless duplication of course content in the four major Chemistry courses.
>
> This realization made it possible for the faculty to withdraw its request for the addition of two new Chemistry courses, because the added rigor provided for existing courses made it possible to achieve better results without adding the new courses.

In several instances, the pilot tests produced rather negative results regarding the target academic program, which led to significant revision of the program. This was the case in such institutions as Trinity College (see Case Study Thirteen) and Notre Dame College of Ohio (see Case Study Ten). While the author of the final report from Notre Dame College made the rather telling comment that "small, independent institutions cannot afford continued pilot testing" (More, 1983b), one cannot help but wonder whether collegiate institutions can "afford" not to pilot test. In the case of Notre Dame College and other QUE colleges, pilot testing resulted in the decision to significantly modify their target academic programs. If this decision had not been made, one wonders what would have been the "cost" to the institution in terms of declining student and/or faculty morale, ill-spent resources, or unmet student, faculty, or administrative expectations. We can never answer this question directly but should keep it in mind when considering the costs associated with conducting and evaluating pilot projects.

꧁꧂ **7** ꧁꧂

Implementing and Evaluating
the Program

At this final phase of the academic planning process, the planning committee at each college or university will face its own unique set of problems and must adopt its own particular set of formal and informal procedures to gain formal approval for the target academic program and to move it to full-scale implementation. Little of a general nature can be said about this phase; hence, this chapter is considerably shorter than those that describe the four previous phases. We also have fewer examples to offer from Project QUE colleges, for the lessons learned at each of these institutions usually are unique to the colleges' own idiosyncratic political and academic cultures.

Phase Five contains three emphases: implementation, continued evaluation, and identification of other programs in the college or university that can be revised or newly created through the academic planning process. The process will not necessarily be applied to other programs in exactly the same manner as to the original target academic program. In fact, academic planners are urged to modify the process according to what was learned from the initial experience and the nature of the newly selected program. However, we do believe that this process comprises basic steps that are valuable to curricular review and revision at any level or magnitude.

Step One: Obtaining Formal
Approval for the Target Academic Program

- *Responsibilities*
  The planning committee prepares the formal proposal for implementation of the target academic program as refined

150

through pilot testing. One or more campus governance bodies review and approve the proposal.

- *Tasks to Be Accomplished*
    1. Prepare a formal proposal for implementation of the target academic program as designed in step seven of Phase Four.
    2. Collect, prepare, sequence, and/or catalogue documents in support of the proposal.
    3. Submit the proposal and accompanying documentation to the appropriate campus governance body or bodies for formal approval.
    4. Testify, lobby, and provide staff support for the formal review of the proposal until it is approved.
    5. Formally acknowledge and celebrate approval of the target academic program.

Choosing an Appropriate Strategy to Gain Approval. In this culminating phase of target academic program development, a planning committee is first faced with the job of obtaining formal institutional approval for implementation of the target program as revised during Phase Four. If the committee has done its homework during the second, third, and fourth phases, the campus is fully aware of the academic program and various design decisions concerning it. Hopefully, many of the campus constituencies also feel some ownership for these design decisions and for the target academic program as a whole. In these cases, the first step of Phase Five will require little effort. In other cases, a planning committee may have chosen to work in relative isolation from other campus constituencies. There may be only minimal awareness of the target academic program, and few people other than those on the planning committee may feel any ownership for the program. For these committees, this first step may be quite difficult and crucial to the success of the target academic program.

Pilot tests can often be done with little outside hassle. New design ideas can be bandied about with little overt opposition. At the point of formal approval for a new target academic program, however, strong opposition often seems to come out of the woodwork. To overcome this opposition, careful attention must be given to a variety of different strategies for promotion of the new program: (1) rational, (2) political, (3) informal, and (4) participative. These four strategies were briefly described in Chapter Three with reference to the original selection of a target academic program (Phase One). They are just as appropriate for Phase Five approval of the fully designed program.

With reference to rational strategies, we suggest that the planning committee accumulate its evaluation data from the Phase Four pilot tests and present these data in a persuasive document that accompanies the formal proposal. This document should balance qualitative and quantitative information. In many instances, a case study, series of quotations, or sequence of descriptive vignettes is as convincing to faculty from a variety of disciplines as descriptive statistics (means, medians, standard deviations, frequency distributions) or more sophisticated statistical analyses (correlations, chi squares, analyses of variance, multiple-regression analyses, factor analyses).

A political strategy is particularly appropriate at this stage in the academic planning process. While each campus has its own political traditions, structures, and processes, planning committee members should be encouraged to link the target academic program with other special interests and projects on campus. Each constituency should be able to identify one or more immediate benefits of the target academic program. At Olivet College (Michigan), plans were developed early in Phase Five for the integration of their target program ("Communication Across the Curriculum") into the academic program of the college. They tied their plan closely to a newly proposed freshman core program that has the teaching of communication skills as its primary function. By tying these two new programs together— with each complementing the other—the Olivet QUE planning committee hoped to improve its chances of gaining campus acceptance of the target program. The Olivet planning committee also decided to present a proposal that was broader than just acceptance of its target program. The committee asked the faculty for broad-based support of the communication-skills component of the college's curriculum. The faculty approved this proposal and committed themselves to teaching communication skills in their courses at Olivet. If the planning committee does not represent all important campus constituencies, this might be an appropriate time to invite other "friends" of the target program to assist in preparation of the formal proposal and supporting documentation. Their presence during this phase of program planning may enhance credibility as well as inject the process with new perspectives and insights.

The informal approach to promotion of the target academic program suggests an emphasis on one-on-one contact and communication with influential campus leaders. The planning committee might wish to host informal social events, celebrating the completion of the first four phases of the project and the movement toward full-scale implementation. Committee members should be particularly sensitive at this point to people on campus who have made a contribution to the development of the target academic program. By formally acknowledging this contribution or by sending out notes of appreciation, a planning committee is increasing support for the target program.

The fourth strategy—participation—suggests the preparation of target academic program proposals and documents in cooperation with those members of the campus community who must approve the proposal. Perhaps the academic dean, the chair of the faculty senate or curriculum committee, or the division chairpersons should be invited to a meeting of the committee for a discussion of procedures to be followed in preparing and submitting the proposal. People who have opposed the project or continue to have serious reservations about the target academic program might be brought in for one final discussion about ways in which the target program currently addresses or (with minimal revision) could address their concerns.

Preparing a Formal Proposal. A formal proposal—the first task for step one—should convey the essence of the project and the target program without becoming bogged down in details. The proposal should build on the target academic program design prepared during the final step of Phase Four (Chapter Six). In most instances, the proposal need not be very elaborate.

In completing the second task, the committee should prepare documentation that is responsive to the four strategies described above. A variety of documents should be prepared: reports, letters of support, transcripts, memorandums, photographs, videotapes, and so forth. If more than a half-dozen documents accompany the proposal, a brief description of these documents (annotated table of contents) should accompany and precede them, so that readers will not be turned off by the volume of documents presented and so that they become aware of the type of documentation that is being presented.

Presenting the Proposal. When the proposal and accompanying documents are presented to the appropriate governing body for approval, an oral hearing might be requested—even if this is not traditionally done at the college or university. Members of the committee can describe not only the target academic program but also the general nature of the Academic Planning Model. In some instances, formal discussions and negotiations about the target academic program will lead to modification in the design or even to the implementation of additional pilot tests. If a new program is to be successful, campuswide ownership usually is necessary prior to its full-scale implementation. This expanded ownership often requires extraordinary tolerance on the part of people who have been working on the program for some time. They must stand aside temporarily to let other people incorporate their own goals and ideas. Effectively designed academic planning projects often falter at this point because of the unwillingness of some to "abandon their baby." Heavily invested members of the planning committee might wish to play a secondary role at this point, possibly directing their attention to some other project while the target academic program is being deliberated.

After formal approval is received for full-scale implementation, we urge a moment of reflection and celebration, as well as formal acknowledgment of the program's approval. Sensitivity to the contributions made by many people in the successful preparation of this new program is particularly important at this time. The support and assistance of many people are usually needed as the planning committee moves toward full-scale implementation of the target academic program.

Step Two: Planning for Full-Scale
Implementation of the Target Academic Program

- *Responsibilities*
  The faculty and administrators who will actually be implementing the target academic program develop the plans in conjunction with the planning committee.
- *Tasks to be Accomplished*
  1. Identify the resources that will be needed to implement the target academic program.
  2. Identify means for obtaining, creating, selecting, and/or upgrading needed resources.
  3. Identify ways of linking the target academic program with other existing programs on campus, so that the target program might be assisted by these other programs and might enable them to function more effectively.

Identifying Needed Resources. Having obtained formal approval for the target academic program, the planning committee will usually want to pass the primary responsibility for planning its full-scale implementation to the people who will actually be running it. The committee should turn its attention to the activities in steps five and six of Phase Five. Those who will be implementing the target program must review the resources they will need: (1) How many faculty are needed? (2) How much and what type of administrative/clerical support is needed? (3) How many and what type of students are needed for this program to be successful? (4) What should be the budget for this program? Where will this budget be housed? (5) How much and what kind of space is required? (6) What kind of equipment is needed, how often is it needed, and when is it needed? (7) What is the time schedule for this program? How often will activities be conducted and for what duration? While the answers to most of these questions will have been determined previously, some may require a level of detail that has not been provided before. Often some further negotiation and decision making are required at this point. The planning committee may have to intervene and lend support regarding budgetary requirements, staffing requests, and so forth.

With the identification of resources, program implementers must identify means by which these resources can be obtained or created. As some resources will have to be selected from among several alternative candidates, selection criteria must be developed. Implementers should also begin to develop plans for maintenance and upgrading of resources. What kind of professional development activities will the implementers adopt so that they might improve or sustain relevant skills and bases of knowledge? A number of excellent books are available to provide direction for faculty and administrative development efforts: *A Handbook for Faculty Development*, Volumes 1, 2, and 3 (Bergquist and Phillips, 1975, 1977, 1981); *Institutional Renewal Through the Improvement of Teaching* (Gaff, 1978); *Designing Teaching Improvement Programs* (Lindquist, 1978a); *Improving Teaching Styles* (Eble, 1980); *Effective Approaches to Faculty Development* (Nelsen and Siegel, 1980); and *Handbook for College Administration* (Sprunger and Bergquist, 1978).

Relating to Other Programs. Finally, in preparing for the full-scale target academic program, the implementers need to identify other ongoing campus programs with which the target academic program can be linked. The implementers need only look around campus to discover one or more other programs that relate in some direct manner to the target academic program. Frequently, innovators in higher education work in isolation from one another, thereby increasing the possibility of competing for available resources, alternative campus goals, student interests, and so forth. The isolation among innovators also contributes to their burnout as effective advocates and practitioners. The linkages among new programs on a campus are often essential to their survival.

As a program that was selected, in part, for its "enabling" quality, the target academic program ought to be of value to other programs on campus. These benefits should be identified by the target academic program implementers in collaboration with the leaders of other campus programs, and plans should be made to ensure that these benefits are sustained. In addition, ways should be found for the target academic program implementers to derive benefits from other campus projects, and plans should be made for the continuation of these benefits.

What types of mutual benefits are possible? First, scarce resources can be shared. For example, an expensive piece of equipment might be jointly purchased. Second, two or more program units might cooperate in off-campus promotion of activities and recruitment of new students. Third, expertise can be shared between programs. This expertise might be content specific, method specific, or related more generally to the initiation, management, and/or evaluation of a new program. Fourth, the various program leaders can support and sustain each other under the difficult conditions associated with starting any new program. Periodic meetings might be scheduled during which problems are discussed and collaboratively solved. Some mutual support might also be offered, with each program leader agreeing to back up other program leaders when presentations or requests must be made to the general campus community or to some off-campus constituency. While competition between programs might be necessary at some point, it should be minimized. This aspect of Phase Five will be complemented by the planning committee's attention in step five to other on-campus uses of the Academic Planning Model.

Step Three: Ongoing Monitoring and Periodic Judging of the Target Academic Program

- *Responsibilities*
  Faculty and administrators who will be implementing the target academic program prepare plans for evaluation in conjunction with one or more program evaluation specialists (on or off campus).
- *Tasks to Be Accomplished*
  1. Determine the formative (monitoring) and summative (judging) evaluation needs for the full-scale target academic program.
  2. Review the effectiveness of previous efforts during Phase Four.

3. Design an evaluation plan for the target academic program, based on identified needs and previous evaluation experiences.

Before full-scale implementation of the target academic program is begun, one additional planning activity must be completed. An evaluation program must be designed that will enable those who are running the program to continually monitor and improve it and that will enable various campus leaders to receive periodic reports concerning its success in meeting both specified and unspecified outcomes. These tasks should be accomplished by those implementing the target academic program in conjunction with the planning committee and, possibly, with the assistance of people on or off campus who are knowledgeable about program evaluation.

Identifying Researchable Questions. First, the implementers should decide what questions they need answered on a regular basis for internal use (formative evaluation). These questions might concern (1) student satisfaction with the program, (2) ways in which students think that the program can be improved, (3) the perceptions of other campus constituencies about the program while it is being implemented, (4) the costs of specific program units in terms of money, time, and/or space, and (5) the benefits of specific program units in terms of learning outcomes, student interests, institutional reputation, and so on.

Second, the implementers should identify those questions that important campus constituencies (for example, the academic dean, faculty senate, trustees) want the program staff to address on a periodic basis. These questions might concern (1) student learning outcomes, (2) the attractiveness of the program to prospective students, (3) the success of students who have "graduated" from the program in terms of their subsequent education or career advancement, (4) the overall costs of the target program as compared to the costs of comparable programs on campus or at other colleges or universities, and (5) the overall level of campus awareness of and support for the target academic program.

As in the previous phases, the program implementers and planning committee members during Phase Five should determine which of the questions that have been generated are researchable and which require further deliberation or clarification concerning values, goals, or attitudes. Those questions that are not immediately researchable need either to be addressed outside the evaluation process or to be reformulated so that they do become researchable. A question such as "Is this academic program successful?" must be reformulated with reference to its success in achieving specific goals.

The first list of questions that has been generated concerning the internal management of the program should dictate the design of an ongoing formative evaluation process for the academic program. The second set of questions, addressing the needs of people outside the target academic program, should dictate the design of a periodic summative evaluation process for the target program (see Bergquist and Armstrong, 1985)

Learning from Phase Four Experiences. If formative evaluation was conducted during Phase Four, then the planning committee already should have rather extensive experience with the planning and implementation of program evaluation. The lessons learned from the Phase Four evaluation should be reviewed before Phase Five evaluation plans become firm. Following is a list of questions that might be asked about the Phase Four evaluation:

1. What type of question was addressed successfully during Phase Four? What type of question could not be addressed successfully? What are the implications of these successes and failures for Phase Five evaluations?
2. What type of Phase Four evaluation information was most helpful in formulating the final design for the target academic program? What type of evaluative information was least helpful? What are the implications of these findings for Phase Five evaluations?
3. What were the positive and negative reactions of Phase Four participants to the evaluation procedure that was used? How

can the negative reactions be avoided and positive reactions be increased during the Phase Five evaluation?

4. Which were the most valuable evaluation resources (people, instruments, equipment, and so on) used during Phase Four? How can they be employed during the Phase Five evaluation?

5. What did we fail to evaluate during Phase Four that we would like to evaluate during Phase Five?

Designing the Formative Evaluation Program. The ongoing formative evaluation process must be realistic and sensitive to the limited resources available. Frequently, formative evaluations are initiated that cannot be sustained after the initial enthusiasm and goodwill wear off. A plan must be derived that can be sustained and supported in the future by people who might not be excited about either evaluation or the target academic program. Two or three basic sources of information should be identified that provide several different perspectives on the target academic program and that involve several different methodologies (questionnaires, observations, performance, testing, and so on).

The most comprehensive formative evaluation project among the QUE colleges was probably that at the College of St. Teresa (Minnesota), which focused on the context in which the target program (core curriculum) was conducted, the input into the program, the process of the program, and the program's product. At the implementation stage, the evaluation was chiefly process oriented, while context was dominant during the early years, when attention focused on institutional priorities, assessment of needs, and surveys of faculty, alumni, and student attitudes. The input phase was completed during the first two years of the project, when most of the pilot testing of program components was initiated. The product of the program is studied semiannually through documentation of the objectives and their achievement in the core curriculum at St. Teresa. All of this information feeds into the decision-making processes of the college regarding this central element of the institution's curriculum.

Designing the Summative Evaluation Program. A summative evaluation should be planned for no more than once a year and preferably no more than once every three to five years. Infrequent reports from carefully conceived summative evaluations are more likely to be read and used than are frequent reports from an "overevaluated" program. The time and energy being diverted from the program to the evaluation must also be taken into account.

At the College of St. Teresa, summative evaluation of the target academic program is built on the assessment of several independent criteria for judging whether the program is successful and effective. The implementation team and a "Triangular Council" (composed of the dean of academic affairs, the dean of students, and the pastoral team director) assess the extent to which each of these criteria is met. Their assessment, in turn, is based in part on results from a summative evaluation questionnaire that is distributed to students and another that is distributed to faculty, student affairs personnel, members of the pastoral team, and administrators at the college. While the formative and summative evaluation procedures at the College of St. Teresa are much more elaborate than those found at other QUE colleges, they point to the value of a systematic, thoughtfully conceived evaluation program. Most of the assessments that have been done for either formative or summative purposes at the College of St. Teresa could easily be done by other colleges and universities that wish to systematically monitor and improve the quality of central academic programs.

Selecting Members of the Evaluation Teams. A summative evaluation should, in most cases, involve one or more people from off campus, as well as someone on campus who is not directly affiliated with the target academic program. Major expenses can be avoided if the outside evaluator is a trustee, a "friend of the college," or a faculty member or administrator from a sister institution (usually in the same consortium or higher education system).

For the formative evaluation, those who are implementing the target program need not look off campus. Members of

the evaluation team can all come from one's own campus, unless
the target program is highly controversial or involves virtually
everyone on campus (as is the case, for example, with some
general education programs). An on-campus formative evaluation team might consist of one or more faculty members, mid-
level administrators, faculty or administrator spouses, and members of the clerical staff. While the team should include at least
one person with program evaluation experience (not just background in behavioral science research), not all members of the
team need this experience. They can learn "on the job"—
especially if the formative evaluation is done frequently.
Members of the team might serve for several years on an over-
lapping basis.

Identifying the Client and Audience. The evaluation plan
should identify not only the formative and summative evaluation team members but also the "client" and "audience" for
each evaluation. The client for a formative evaluation is usually
one or more of the people who are running the target program.
The audience for a formative evaluation is composed of those
people who will receive copies of all formative reports that are
prepared. The audience may influence the type of evaluation
questions that are asked and methods that are used but serve
in an advisory rather than decision-making capacity. The academic dean, the president, and members of major faculty and
student committees are usually included in the audience for a
formative evaluation.

The client for a summative evaluation, by contrast, is the
person or group to whom those implementing the target program are responsible: the academic dean, curriculum committee, division chair, and so forth. The audience for a summative
evaluation often is the general campus committee, the board
of trustees, friends of the college or university, and—if the target
academic program is particularly interesting or successful—the
higher education community.

Formulating Evaluation Plans. The evaluation plans should
include listings of activities and anticipated outcomes, assignments of task responsibilities, time schedules, and the identification of means for periodic evaluation of the evaluative processes

that are being used. Perhaps most importantly, the evaluation plan should contain simple and direct statements about the purposes for each component of the plan. This statement should be conveyed to each person that participates in any aspect of either the formative or summative evaluation. The purposes of both evaluations should be perceived as constructive and sensitive to the goals of the target academic program and the mission of the college or university.

Step Four: Implementing the Full-Scale Target Academic Program

- *Responsibilities*
  The faculty and administrators implementing the target academic program work in consultation with members of the planning committee.
- *Tasks to Be Accomplished*
  1. Implement the target academic program.
  2. Conduct formative and summative evaluations of the target academic program as appropriate.
  3. Periodically review and revise the target academic program, on the basis of the evaluations that have been conducted, recycling (if necessary) to components of Phases Three and Four.

At this step in the academic planning process, one of its ultimate goals has been achieved: the target academic program is about to be fully implemented. The full-scale implementation may seem anticlimactic; yet it is the source of considerable gratification for those who have labored hard for this moment. Congratulations are in order.

Cycling Through the Academic Planning Process. There is more to be said at this point, however, without detracting from the importance of full-scale implementation. This planning process is a cycle—a continuing process that never comes to an end. While a linear planning process would conclude at the point of implementation, a cyclical process suggests ongoing planning and a continuing refinement and improvement of program elements through use of the same concepts and procedures that aided in the initial design.

By means of the formative and (to a lesser extent) the summative evaluations, academic program implementers will be able to periodically review and modify program elements. Those elements that are found to be unsatisfactory can be redesigned, using Phase Three procedures and instruments, and/or subjected to further pilot tests, as described in Phase Four. Those elements that are satisfactory always can be improved further through continuing design work that seeks to move closer to the ideal that was identified during Phase Three.

Redefining Ideal Program Design and Goals. Alternatively, implementers of the target academic program may wish to redefine the ideal design and/or the goals, objectives, and desired outcomes of the target academic program in response to further experiences with the program or a sense of changing student, institutional, or societal needs. With a redefined direction for the target academic program, those who run the program may wish to engage in various needs assessment, outcome definition, and design activities from Phases Two and Three. None of this recycling to previous planning phases requires a major disruption in the ongoing activities of the target academic program, nor is much effort required for occasional review of program elements or the overall goals of the program. Periodic reviews of this type are part of any sound program management process and are necessary in any college or university that is exposed to changing conditions inside and outside the institution. The Academic Planning Model provides concepts and procedures that will make this review process more efficient and constructive.

Step Five: Identifying Other Potential
Academic Programs for High Quality Development

- *Responsibilities*
  The committee, in conjunction with other campus leaders, initiates the process. A new planning committee is constituted to continue this process—preferably with one or more

members of the initial committee continuing as members of the new committee.
* *Tasks to Be Accomplished*
  1. Review the academic planning process as it was used for development of the initial target academic program.
  2. Establish a new academic planning process, on the basis of review of the process used for the initial target program.
  3. Implement the new academic planning process.

Just as we suggested the continuing use of planning process resources for the target academic program after it has been implemented, we also suggest use of the entire planning process in other academic areas when (or even before) the initial target academic program is implemented. In this fifth step of Phase Five, we encourage the planning committee and other leaders of the college or university to identify additional academic programs that might be created or improved using this planning process or a revision of it. Three tasks need to be accomplished for this to take place.

Revising the Academic Planning Process. First, the planning committee, in conjunction with other campus leaders, should review the planning process as it took place with regard to the initial target academic program. The following questions should be addressed:

1. Which aspects of the academic planning process that was used for the initial target academic program seemed to be most successful? Why? Which were least successful? Why?
2. What was learned from the initial academic program development process about how change takes place at this college or university? What are the implications of this learning for a revised planning process?
3. What is being learned about academic planning from the relative success or failure of the initial target academic program as it is now being implemented? If we could do it over again, how could we improve planning for our initial target academic program?

4.   In what ways, if any, was the initial academic program different from other academic programs that might be selected
for development? Should any of these differences be taken
into account when reviewing the academic planning process?
5.   In what ways did the academic planning process used at
this institution differ from that suggested in this book?
Should any of the unused concepts, procedures, or instruments be incorporated in the revised planning process?
6.   What conditions at this college or university have changed
since the academic planning process was initiated that would
necessitate changes in this process for the institution?

Redesigning the Planning Process. When these questions (as
well as those that are unique to a college or university) have
been answered, attention should shift to the second task: redesign
of the academic planning process for the institution. In the
accomplishment of this redesign, members of the campus community should have answers to the questions listed above, as
well as one or more copies of this book. At least one or two of
the participants in a discussion on academic planning should
be familiar with the concepts and procedures we have described
herein.

At many Project QUE colleges, steps have been taken to
apply the Academic Planning Model to other campus projects.
An international business program, for instance, has been initiated at Marymount Manhattan College (New York), using
many of the steps in the planning model outlined in this book.
A team of faculty representing business management, foreign
languages, and international studies worked together in collecting and analyzing research data about a sequence of courses,
as well as the needs of the student body. This planning group
wrote a successful grant for funding of the new program that
outlined needs, outcomes, and steps to development of the
program.

At the College of St. Teresa (Minnesota), which used the
QUE project to revise its entire core curriculum, elements of
the Academic Planning Model have been used since the conclusion of Project QUE to further revise and improve the com-

ponents of its core program. The specific steps that were adapted for use in future planning at the College of St. Teresa include: (1) the use of coordinating committees, (2) speculation about possible alternative forms of the program, (3) balancing of idealistic and realistic forms of the programs, (4) careful monitoring through pilot testing, (5) assessment of available resources and priorities of the institution relative to the adoption of the new programs, (6) careful planning to move the innovation through the required approving bodies, and (7) inclusion of formal internal and external dissemination strategies within the formative (monitoring) evaluation procedure.

At Notre Dame College of Ohio, experiences in the QUE project led to some "soul searching" about the way academic planning is usually done at the college and to new planning procedures (More, 1983a, p. 2): "What we learned from our biggest failure, communication breakdown and lack of ownership, was considered in the development of several new programs this year. We changed tactics to increase the sense of faculty that they did have more information on what was happening."

The one specific element in the Academic Planning Model that seems to have taken hold at the greatest number of QUE colleges is the specification of student learning outcomes early in the planning process. King's College (New York) is converting its 1967 general education "Goals for the Student" into outcome statements as a result of the QUE experience, while Dominican College of Blauvelt (New York) has restated the educational objectives in its mission statement in terms of expected outcomes. These outcome statements have become part of Dominican College's master plan and are reviewed annually by the long-range planning team at the college. Each division of the college has developed a set of overall expected outcomes, with outcome specification becoming a central ingredient in planning for new courses in the computer information systems, nursing, teacher education, and business administration departments.

Similarly, at Huntington College (Indiana), student learning outcome statements have been formulated for its new two- and four-year computer science programs, while outcome statements are also now being considered for use in the college's general education program. For the faculty at Neumann College (Pennsylvania) and Marian College (Indiana), Project QUE acted as a stimulus for thinking about and planning learning experiences in terms of student learning outcomes. Many courses at Neumann College are now being developed and evaluated with regard to specified outcomes, while, at Marian College, all proposals for new courses must contain a statement of expected student learning outcomes when they are submitted to the academic affairs committee of the college.

Beginning Again. When the revised academic planning process has been conceived, the college or university is ready to embark on another venture, with a new set of potentials and problems. Hopefully, you and your colleagues will have a better sense about how these problems might be addressed than you did when first engaging in this academic planning process. We believe—and have found ample justification through the experiences of Project QUE—that the academic planning process described in this book can help a college or university achieve its educational mission and meet the changing needs of its students and our society in a systematic and effective manner.

𝕾𝖝𝖝 8 𝕾𝖝𝖝

Using the Planning Model
to Facilitate
Academic Change

Over a four-year period, several million dollars of W. K. Kellogg Foundation, Council of Independent Colleges, and college money and hundreds of thousands of hours of labor were devoted to this project on educational improvement. What did we learn about the processes of planning and change, and about the people and institutions engaged in these processes, that could be of value to others laboring in the vineyards of academic reform?

Somewhat perplexing to us was our own conclusion that we did not learn much about change that was brand new. On the one hand, these findings enable us to affirm with even greater confidence that the higher education community does know quite a bit about the processes of change in an academic setting. We know how to stimulate change and how to facilitate change once it has begun. On the other hand, our findings confront us with the fact that we continue to ignore much of the information that we already have. Thus, some of the observations in this chapter confirm what we have known in higher education for some time. Others, hopefully, add some new insights. We would like these observations to give all of us new confidence in the application of the knowledge we have about improving the quality of education on our own campuses.

We will first address ourselves to the question of what we have learned about the successful planning of academic programs. Attention will then focus on what we have learned about

169

the processes of successful academic change. Finally, we turn to the question of what we have learned about the role of interinstitutional cooperation in successful academic reform.

Successful Planning of Academic Programs

Learning a Planning Model. An objective of paramount importance to the Council of Independent Colleges was that not only should the Project QUE colleges develop a particular program to a new level of quality but also a nucleus of key faculty and administrators should learn a systematic approach to educational program development that would be integrated into the institution's planning process. Was this accomplished? It was in many cases. Thus, we learned that a more systematic approach to planning than had been used heretofore on most campuses can be learned by campus personnel and applied to a variety of programs.

The final report from one college stated:* ''The overall impact of using the structured planning model was not only positive, but pervasive. There is evident increased faculty involvement in curriculum planning and a heightened sensitivity to process. Moreover, an unintended consequence is that strategic planning has begun to occur across various levels of the academic program with several cycles of planning happening simultaneously.'' Another project coordinator wrote: ''In general the most important piece of knowledge our institution has gained from participation in the Project is the awareness of the effective planning model which has been developed by Project QUE. Following this model helped us to plan effectively, to pilot-test and refine and to implement when the time and conditions were 'right.' We believe the Planning Model contributed significantly to the success of our program. We have begun to use the QUE model for program development when initiating new programs or changing existing programs.''

*We are not providing references for the quotations in this chapter because most of them come from sections of the reports written by project coordinators and academic deans where candor was elicited. We believe that the insights contained in these quotations will stand on their own without reference to a particular institution or person.

On the other hand, there is the president that told a project external evaluator that it had not occurred to him to use the model with any other programs. This president never attended a project event and was not much involved with his own campus team. Yet, largely through the efforts of a highly energetic faculty coordinator and several colleagues, this college developed an effective program, even though that one program appears to have been the extent of the direct application of the planning model. Yet another coordinator stated that "recognition of the value of planned program development by a large portion of the faculty was the most important piece of knowledge gained by the college and portions of the model have been applied to seven other programs."

Selecting an Academic Program for Intensive Development. A college's or university's general reputation for high quality often can be traced to a small number of particularly successful academic programs. Developing high-quality academic programs requires considerable resources (time, money, materials, creativity). A college or university cannot engage, therefore, in the intensive development of several high-quality academic programs simultaneously unless it is exceptionally large and has extensive resources. One specific program (a target program) should be carefully selected for focal attention at any one time.

The concept of "enablement" (that is, one program's potential for enabling other programs to be developed or improved) helps a planning group break through the deadlock that often accompanies deliberations regarding which of several important projects should be given highest priority. Rather than just considering the specific, independent importance of each project, a planning group should take a "systems" perspective—considering not just each program's isolated merit but also the effect its success would have in enabling other projects to be developed to a level of high quality.

Identifying Outcomes for an Academic Program. The cornerstone of the planning model was the use of *student learning outcomes* in designing educational programs. We learned that a systematic, outcomes-oriented process of program design can be accepted and learned by many faculty in traditional academic institutions without an unusual expenditure of time or effort.

Some embraced the outcomes concept rapidly; others had to be encouraged constantly to "stick with it." Some had to be pulled and pushed through use of the concept, and several colleges left the project because of lack of enthusiasm for the idea. However, four years of experience with the colleges, external evaluation of their progress, and reports from the various campuses demonstrate that several hundred college faculty members and administrators learned to think about the purpose of their institutions and educational programs in terms of specific educational outcomes for students. A statement by one external evaluator provides evidence: "I was surprised at the lack of resistance among faculty to the behavioral language in which the planning model is couched. Faculty spoke freely and easily about learning outcomes. There is a serious effort to measure programs in this regard and there is unanimity concerning the importance of this goal." At another college, the project coordinator states: "A significant core of faculty has been involved extensively in the process of developing student learning outcome statements. This approach has been very helpful and is being applied to several programs. In the successful preparation of a Title III grant proposal, the outcomes approach was used extensively."

In a project the magnitude of QUE, however, it is probably too much to hope to accomplish 100 percent success with even a central concept. In one external evaluator interview with a faculty member, the following comment emerged: "Most faculty here would not be so oriented [to student learning outcomes]—certainly not to the extent to which the whole QUE program emphasizes this. At the Fall Faculty Retreat, the faculty did talk a bit about these issues. They could readily see the need for writing competencies and math competencies. But in terms of taking a *regular* course—such as history, or one in philosophy—and then seeking to identify various skills and/or competencies (intellectual, vocational, social, or whatever) linked to such courses, plus mapping a program to help our students attain these skills, this approach has not taken hold here."

One thing we learned is that writing student learning outcomes for programs and courses is hard work. Moreover, the term itself gives some people trouble. For some, *objectives* or *goals* is more acceptable. Regardless of what they are called, they need to be written in a way that gives clarification to the mission of an institution and to the purpose of a program or course, and in a way that enables students to know whether they have accomplished them.

Four years ago, the outcomes approach was not widely used to clarify learning expectations and enhance learning results. The National Center for Higher Education Management Systems (NCHEMS) had provided excellent leadership on the outcomes topic, as had the Council for Adult and Experiential Learning (CAEL). Materials authored by J. Marvin Cook for CAEL served as important references for sections of the project manual and workshop sessions on outcomes. We are pleased, in retrospect, that we made use of these latter resources.

The outcomes approach still is not very widely used. However, accrediting associations and state boards of higher education are beginning to emphasize the use of outcomes in program development and evaluation. For example, the new program proposal guidelines for the University of Maine system require listing of learning outcomes as the first item, and Title III guidelines specify incorporation of outcomes-oriented objectives throughout any proposal. In conclusion, this design component did take hold with most colleges in Project QUE. We believe that Project QUE colleges have provided important leadership in demonstrating the feasibility and validity of using outcome statements to improve the quality of education.

Application of *student development principles* was a second foundation stone of the project, as originally conceived. Student development concepts have not been highlighted in this book, since it concerns the processes of academic planning, rather than its content. Additional information about the application of student development concepts to teaching and learning is to be found in four excellent books: *Applying New Developmental Findings* (Knefelkamp, Widick, and Parker, 1978); *Encouraging Development in College Students* (Parker, 1978); *Educating Learners of All Ages* (Greenberg, O'Donnell, and Bergquist, 1980); and *The Modern American College: Responding to the New Realities of Diverse Students and a Changing Society* (Chickering and Associates,

1981). An excellent summary statement on student development was prepared by Joanne Kurfiss (Weber State College, Ogden, Utah), a consultant to Project QUE (Bergquist and Armstrong, 1985).

We developed even stronger opinions about the importance of student development concepts during the past four years. Many QUE colleges made a beginning at applying student development knowledge and principles to teaching and demonstrated that academic programs and approaches to teaching can be more successful when they are designed with sensitivity to the diverse developmental tasks that confront students and to students' varying skills, different learning styles, and varied developmental stages. But we also learned about the vast lack of awareness of and sometimes lack of interest in student development knowledge at institutions of higher education. Throughout the project, workshops and printed materials addressed this issue. Because "student development" is often confused with "student affairs," "student personnel work," or even remedial activities ("developmental studies"), the cognitive, intellectual, and ethical development theories of Jean Piaget (Inhelder and Piaget, 1958) and William Perry (1968) were emphasized in Project QUE. We wanted to demonstrate that student development concerns the "hard" (thinking) as well as "soft" (feeling) aspects of student life.

Project QUE was the first national curriculum development program to stress the critical importance of incorporating knowledge of cognitive development in curriculum and instructional planning. In addition to being a pioneer in this effort, the project began at a time when little literature existed on the actual application of this theoretical knowledge in the classroom. How does one design courses and employ teaching methods differently to take advantage of what is known about student development? The understanding of how to use student development knowledge has progressed since the start of Project QUE; however, it is still in its infancy. That can be changed only if faculty experiment with this knowledge as they design their courses and plan their teaching methodologies.

Many faculty participating in Project QUE changed their teaching after learning about such student development concepts as "dualistic and multiplistic thinking" (Perry, 1968), "concrete and formal operations" (Inhelder and Piaget, 1958), and "challenge and support" (Sanford, 1966). Others became intrigued with David Kolb's (1981, 1984) learning styles concepts. It is clear to us that student development and learning styles knowledge has its greatest potential for enhancing learning through altering how teachers teach. While it is more difficult to identify structural changes that have been made in courses or programs, the changes made by some faculty in their approaches to teaching and in their attitudes about students who are less developed cognitively are encouraging and foreshadow, we believe, incorporation of this knowledge into course and curricular design.

To us, the project demonstrated that there is no greater need in higher education today than improvement in faculty understanding of the relationship between cognitive development and student learning. That understanding is minimal at our colleges and universities, and until that condition is changed, our institutions will continue their failure to foster major improvements in human learning. Student development concepts can make a difference. At a time when concern over educational problems pervades our society, an important potential contributor to solutions is being ignored. The expansion of attention to how students learn and concurrent attention to how we teach can make a difference in the quality of education. Such a focus on the teaching/learning process is still lacking, and financial support from foundations and educational systems is still badly needed to help create this focus.

Designing an Academic Program. A major feature of the design phase was the development of a program in its *ideal form*, rather than starting with the realistic considerations and limiting factors that so often dictate the shape of a new program. Academic programs can be designed more imaginatively—and tend to be more successful—if emphasis is placed throughout the design process (or at least at the start of this process) on ideal as well as realistic parameters. Exclusive emphasis at the start of a design process on realism (about resources, precedence, and acceptability to other faculty, students, administrators, and trustees) prematurely limits the generation of ideas that may be quite practical once given full consideration.

Pilot Testing an Academic Program. Before fully implementing a newly designed or redesigned academic program, a faculty member or planning group should find a way to pilot test the program (or, at least, elements of the program and related teaching methods) without risking significant disruption in learning, faculty or student morale, or the college's or university's reputation. The method used to pilot test these elements must ensure ongoing program evaluation and modification and must allow for some experimentation and risk of error. Pilot testing an academic program, a course, or a set of courses was another curricular design component that was foreign to many faculty members participating in Project QUE. In general, faculty seem to hold the belief that once they develop the content expertise for a course, they are ready to teach it to those for whom it was designed. In their defense, seldom have faculty been granted the time or financial resources to do otherwise.

The Project QUE staff was concerned that many college faculty and administrators, in the urgency to put a program into action, would attempt to finesse the pilot-testing requirement. This was not the case. Faculty and their administrative supporters saw the value of experimenting with new approaches to teaching and to teaching new content on a small scale prior to implementation with large numbers of students. Widespread agreement developed that learning—through pilot testing— about use of outcomes and student development principles, team teaching, student responses to new content, the integration of field experience into courses, and the use of new teaching methodologies and assessment techniques was critical to successful full-scale implementation of the target program. In fact, some colleges chose to expand pilot testing to a second year as an incremental approach to full implementation.

Implementing and Evaluating an Academic Program. Academic programs are readily implemented after being carefully selected, designed, and pilot tested, but ongoing program evaluation is very difficult to implement at most colleges, because funding is not readily available. Small colleges are painfully deficient in expertise, time, and resources for evaluation. Consequently, even with the assistance of the project, impact on evaluation was modest. Attitudes about the need for evaluation often pose another obstacle. To quote one faculty member who was interviewed: "We *know* that the students are learning more as a result of changes we have made. What more do we want?"

Even when significant progress has been made in changing the attitudes of faculty and administrators about evaluation, the ability to conduct evaluation often continued to be limited in Project QUE colleges as a result of lack of resources and expertise. Furthermore, program evaluation problems are compounded in small institutions, where it is virtually impossible to work with experimental and control groups—since frequently there is an insufficient number of students for two classes to be taught on the same subject. While we emphasized "quasi-experimental" means of assessing outcomes and encouraged program evaluators to go outside traditional experimental modes of evaluation, many QUE colleges prematurely abandoned the task of program evaluation.

The ability to integrate evaluation into program enhancement or development may be markedly different at large universities. Most large institutions have institutional research offices that can provide the time and fiscal resources along with the expertise needed to design and implement evaluation procedures. The critical mass of students available in multiple sections of large university courses also simplifies and purifies the research design. In this component of the planning model, the resources associated with the size of the institution may be quite advantageous.

Despite the obstacles to evaluation, Project QUE assisted many small colleges in designing programs that were more easily subjected to evaluation and convinced many faculty members and administrators of the necessity for systematic evaluation for the purpose of improving programs and communicating the quality of these programs to their constituencies.

The Processes of Successful Academic Change

As stated above, we learned that faculty and staff in our colleges can learn procedures and principles of a new academic planning model that, when applied, can enhance the quality of learning. What did we learn about the factors that are critical to successful change through application of this model?

Influence of the Dominant Organizational Culture of the Institution. Each college or, at large institutions (such as universities), each unit within the institution has created its own unique organizational culture. The accurate assessment of the dominant organizational culture within a college, university, or unit involved in the program development process is critical to—and must precede—the selection of a specific academic planning strategy. The organizational culture is conveyed and sustained through traditions, stories, habits, implicit rewards, and styles of leadership/followership. The culture is more than just the sum of personalities and relationships within the institution. These personalities and relationships, in fact, are strongly influenced by the dominant culture, as are the strategies for academic change.

In an organizational culture that values and builds on cooperation and a sense of community, the processes of consensus building that are embedded in all phases of the Academic Planning Model are of great value, if not indispensable, as a means of ensuring widespread commitment to all elements of an academic program. This culture is most frequently apparent in QUE colleges that are affiliated with churches of a strong congregational heritage. At colleges where the organizational culture encourages and supports the dominant role of a few campus leaders in the design and implementation of academic programs, the consensus-building processes of Project QUE were often irrelevant or even counterproductive. Such is sometimes the case in colleges with a very strong relationship to a church body that has a highly traditional or hierarchical approach to administration. When the organizational culture supports autonomous actions on the part of faculty, administrators, and even students, the consensus-building processes of Project QUE are most appropriate when initiated within specific program units (departments, committees, special project task forces). This autonomous culture was most prevalent in colleges that are secular in origin or are only marginally connected to any religious tradition.

Openness to New Ideas and Belief in Their Importance. The attitudes of those involved in and potentially affected by a new program are, of course, critical to its success and the success of new ideas embedded in the program and new concepts that are related to the development of these new ideas. In Project QUE, great differences existed in campus climate or culture with regard to willingness to consider new program ideas and concepts, capacity to form a commitment to these new ideas, and ability of people to work together on their adoption.

While the program that was selected for development or revision involved educational content (for example, general education, a major, a set of courses, a career planning program), the concepts involved in the developmental model were nondisciplinary and relatively nontraditional in nature. To a great degree, success was correlated with the often discussed "content-centered" versus "student-centered" approaches to teaching (Bergquist, Gould, and Greenberg, 1981, pp. 158–163). Where education focuses primarily on *what* is to be learned by the student, consideration of *how* students learn does not stimulate the enthusiasm needed for restructuring courses and teaching methods. The prevailing attitude is characterized by the comment heard on one campus that "when one has several courses to teach, knowledge in one's discipline to keep up with, and a committee to serve on, there just isn't enough time to give attention to some of these other ideas, as good as they may be."

Yet some communities of scholar-teachers find, or make, the time to examine and adopt new ideas. While usually these institutions are organized by disciplinary departments, interdisciplinary activity exists. At these colleges, there is at least a nucleus of individuals in the liberal arts who think in terms of the *results* or *outcomes* of learning. If "professional" departments exist, often the faculty members in these departments are accustomed to thinking in terms of outcomes. Such institutions often can be described as "student centered," not lacking in rigor related to disciplinary learning but more broadly interested in change in students resulting from the total educational experience and willing to consider how to improve the teaching/learning process.

Dedication. An openness to new ideas and a view of education that goes beyond disciplinary content lead to a dedication to ideas that have been adopted through community consideration. Belief in and excitement about a new program generate the energy required for development. There is no substitute for time and hard work devoted to the creation of high-quality learning experiences.

A sense of shared commitment and the ability to work together also are necessary for increasing the efficiency and effectiveness of the effort. In this regard, the disproportionately high degree of success in the project of Catholic women's colleges or coeducational colleges sponsored by women's orders probably was not an accident. The "religious" among the faculty and staff exist in "communities," and the term has both symbolic and practical significance for effective collaboration within the larger college community. The attraction of others with similar views further enhances that college community's ability to change.

To achieve institutional success, it is imperative that those not directly participating in the change process be involved through receiving frequent communication about its progress. Broad community commitment, as well as the dedication of several individuals, is critical. As dedicated as several persons may be, when the interest of only a small number is sustained, smaller successes and narrower impact result. The vice-president for academic affairs at a QUE college made this point quite forcefully in his final QUE report: "The most important advice we would give to colleagues at another college about to undertake new program development would be to engender a sense of ownership on the part of as many participants as possible. Otherwise, such projects are viewed as something 'they' want to accomplish. The best way to achieve a broad base of involvement is to have an on-going long range planning process that systematically encourages colleagues to plan and to develop priorities."

The planning committee at another QUE college made a similar point in its Phase Three report, referring specifically to the value of the academic planning process in building this ownership: "As the [planning] committee discussed the matter at the workshop in Wittenberg this past summer, it was noted that one of the big mistakes in connection with the [college's] QUE project was the failure to follow the QUE procedures more closely, on the assumption that at least some of them had been adequately covered. Probably the most important issue was revealed during the discussion with the faculty of the two possible core program structures suggested by the QUE committee. Although the faculty had been included in the project at all steps of the process, and although they had actually helped develop and had approved formally the modules and domains, their perceptions were that they did not understand them and that they did not have any ownership in them." With this recognition, the planning committee at this college went on to more actively engage the attention and build the ownership of its faculty for the target program at the college.

Leadership. We have long known that leadership is important. Leadership in any program development effort comes from many different sources. Those who mildly suggest or forcefully state that a need (or deficiency) exists, who initiate planning efforts to improve educational outcomes (what is learned) for students, will vary from campus to campus and, on any campus, from day to day. The voice urging change may be that of a single faculty member or a group of student affairs staff, a president, dean, division chair, department head, student organization, faculty committee, provost, or program director. Usually, whenever the voice emerges, consultation must take place to determine the extent of support, philosophical and/or fiscal, for a change. A president, chair, or provost may say, "It's a good idea, but we don't have the money (or the right people or the facilities) to do it." Yet a determined group of faculty might develop a plan for strengthening a current program or adding a new one, presenting such a persuasive case for the potential benefits of the change that a way is found to implement the change.

In Project QUE, specific but different leadership roles were expected of the president, dean, and campus coordinator. What did we learn about each of these expected roles? Program success was most dependent on leadership from the campus coordinator. Furthermore, the quality of the program reached a higher level where the coordinator was a faculty member who had been given released time rather than a dean who accepted an additional responsibility. Every highly successful program involved a respected, well-organized, committed campus coordinator. Such an individual generated the necessary support and involvement of others. Perhaps the experiences of one of the less successful programs is most telling: "We are not spending enough time on the QUE Project. No one person is giving the overall program sufficient leadership. As [a campus leader] put it, 'We are creating a program which we are unwilling or unable to staff.' Reasons could be given why the QUE coordinator was falling behind in his duties, but they would sound like the usual organizational excuses."

The role of the planning committee was also important—though usually not as important as that of the campus coordinator. Continuity of leadership on the planning committee seemed to be key. For instance, the campus coordinator at one QUE college that experienced considerable difficulty throughout the project comments on the problem of continuity: "A basic problem that has been with us almost since the beginning has been the turnover of membership on the Team. Five of the original team members have left the committee, for any number of reasons. During the fall semester of 1981, we met without a coordinator, and this also set us back. We spent a good part of last year trying to bring the new members into the spirit of what we were doing. Again this year, we are adding two new members, as well as several advisors to the team. A positive effect of this shift in membership has been that many people have been involved with QUE; a negative effect is that it has held us back in our development of the [target program] and its implementation."

There were a few colleges where strong coordinators and planning committees existed but the academic deans lacked enthusiasm. This combination resulted in less success. While today's universities and colleges look to the president for general direction and tone setting, they look to the dean, academic vice-president, or provost (in larger institutions, this may translate to the dean of a college or a division or department chair) for day-to-day encouragement and support of educational activities. In Project QUE, campus teams and programs floundered when the dean did not exhibit active interest in the planning concepts and the target program. On some campuses, a dean was expected to deal with tasks ranging from handling daily administrative minutiae (because of lack of assistance) to serving as internal president. Fragmentation of attention and fatigue reduced involvement with the project. A few deans did not find the planning concepts appealing. In some cases, honest philosophical differences occurred; in others, lack of a broader perspective or imagination existed. Many of the cases of withdrawal from the project can be traced to a failure of project leadership in the dean's office, while the greatest successes involved, on the part of the dean, a high level of interest in the program, support of the project's planning principles and activities, and a comfortable working relationship with the coordinator. To a very large degree, the integration of the planning model into institutional procedures for use in revising or developing other programs depended upon leadership from the dean or chief academic officer. No one else on campus is in the position to continually suggest and support use of the planning process as opportunities arise. From the perspective of the project staff, the most successful institutions were those where this leadership occurred, and it did occur in an encouraging number of cases.

An overriding requisite for campus support of change and subsequent program success is the belief that a new program is central to the institution and significant to its future. Directly or indirectly, the president communicates the degree to which he or she embraces this belief. Herein lies the key to the presidential role. When conceived, the project hypothesized that very active presidential participation would be needed throughout the project. Among the more successful institutions, the level of sustained presidential activity varied. Successful program development, however, was highly correlated with direct involvement of the president in the planning committee during the first one or two years, followed by close communications with the team and visible support of its work during the remainder of the project. In cases where presidents continued to focus on external or financial matters—to the extent that they were perceived as indifferent to or minimally interested in the program under development—only modest success was produced, regardless of the leadership and dedication of others.

While experience showed that less active participation by the president throughout the project was needed for success than originally envisioned, the project clearly demonstrated that the role of the president is critical. For successful program development to occur, the president must show commitment to the idea and to those working on the idea. The timing and style of presidential leadership are important in order to avoid the perception that the president is campaigning for or imposing a particular idea or program on the institution. The planning model used in Project QUE cultivated active involvement of the president but provided consensus-building procedures for program selection and design. Presidents helped get the planning process moving, then permitted academic deans and campus coordinators to lead the process, while continuing to show interest and provide support. In general, other demands on the president did not permit extensive involvement for all four years, but, in conjunction with strong leadership from an academic dean and several faculty members, the strategy just described was quite effective.

A Summary Statement. Project QUE has taught us many things about academic planning within small liberal arts colleges. We believe from our experience in other kinds of colleges and universities that much of what was learned is broadly relevant to contemporary collegiate institutions: a systematic academic planning program can help improve the quality of teaching and learning. Furthermore, this systematic planning is most likely to be successful when (1) campus talent is combined with an openness to new ideas of both content and process, (2) the president, dean, and key faculty and staff members each understand, accept, perform, and coordinate their own distinct leadership roles in the project, (3) some financial support is available, and (4) a special commitment to change is combined with the willingness to invest large amounts of time and hard work in improving the educational program. Whether an institution is public or independent or large, medium, or small in size does not change the applicability of the planning and leadership principles central to this model. This conviction is supported by the authors' experience and the results of other projects involving institutions larger than and different from those in Project QUE. Examples include the Student Outcomes Project of the National Center for Higher Education Management Systems and the Project on General Education Models (Gaff, 1981).

In institutions, public or independent, that are similar in size to those in Project QUE (approximately 2,000 students) or somewhat larger, the plan can be followed much the same way it was in Project QUE. The utility of this model is not related to type of institutional funding or affiliation. How the model is applied or adapted is influenced by organizational structure and culture and by definition of responsibilities assumed by organizational officers, leaders, and members. Small public institutions differ very little, if at all, from small independent institutions with regard to factors that affect the application of the planning model described in this book.

The organizational structure of president, chief academic officers, and divisions, departments, or small schools or colleges within the institution is directly comparable to the organization of most independent liberal arts colleges or "small comprehensive institutions." In a private college, a president's involvement in educational matters often is impeded by fund-raising activities. These are replaced in the life of the president of a public institution by cultivation of legislators and, perhaps, the state system's chancellor. Increasingly, fund-raising and alumni activities occur in the public institution as well. The functions of the chief academic officer, chairs or deans, and faculty committees are parallel to those of counterparts in an independent institution. In fact, we believe that the model could be useful to a variety of organizations outside of higher education. Moreover, although the use of the model in Project QUE focused on academic or curricular planning, by no means is its value limited to that component of educational institutions. Certainly program development in student services or student affairs could benefit from the principles and framework of the model. Many of the principles also could be applied to broader institutional planning.

As institutional size increases to several or many thousands of students, the administrative and faculty structures within a single unit, such as a school or college of the university, will parallel those of an entire small state-supported or independent institution. Most often, in small or large organizations, qualitative change does not take place across the organization through one sweeping initiative. It is produced through focus on development or improvement in a small number of units; sometimes these units are academic, sometimes administrative. At times, the change process involves a single unit or a single theme (for example, general education or career development) across several units, academic and/or nonacademic. At other times, it incorporates several units, independently or interactively. In the authors' experience in a variety of organizations, independent or public, academic or otherwise, simultaneous changes in more than one unit often do not take place with appropriate awareness of, let alone connection with, each other. This model does not automatically solve that problem—only the people using it can do that—but it incorporates steps that, if properly followed, can reduce fragmentation in the planning effort. We believe that the planning principles and processes described in this book and tested in this project can be used to advantage wherever student educational needs must be addressed and people within an organization must organize in some way to address them.

Obviously, the president and chief academic officer usually will not play the same role in a large university as in a small college. For example, in a large university, if the dean and/or some number of faculty members of the college of engineering wish to add a program in electrical engineering, an exploration of broader interest and support must be initiated. That is where the planning process comes in. While the university's provost may function within the planning process much as does the small college president in QUE, the university's president at least should be consulted before large amounts of time and energy are expended on planning a program that may have significant educational impact on the university or call for major new financial resources. In a large university department of psychology, consisting of over one hundred faculty, a major overhaul of the required field or research experience for all majors may be desired. The department chair may function like the "dean" and the dean of arts and sciences like the president in a small college as the planning procedures are followed.

Perhaps the vice-president of student affairs of a university wishes to have student activities and services for older students reviewed and improved. She may appoint the assistant dean for nontraditional students as coordinator of a task force for this purpose. The planning model, although initially designed for "academic programs," is equally relevant to other kinds and as applicable to strengthening current programs as developing new ones.

In a large state college, English department faculty may agree to integrate the use of the computer in selected basic composition and advanced creative writing courses on a trial basis. The funds necessary for faculty training and development are available in a discretionary line item in the department's budget. All that is required before the planning process can begin is the blessing of the liberal arts dean, who in turn enthusiastically informs the academic vice-president of the department's wishes to experiment with new teaching methodologies. In another case, the school of education, which admits students only for the last two years, works with the college of arts, the institute of science and technology, and the office of career development to design and implement major revisions and improvements in the university's academic advising and career counseling programs. The deans or directors of those units appoint an interunit committee chaired by a faculty member with released time to devote to the project, the associate deans of the units as a group of four assume the "dean's" role in the model, and the university provost is comparable to the "president."

The Role of Interinstitutional
Collaboration in Successful Academic Reform

A cosmopolitan perspective among faculty involved in reform is highly important to the success of that reform. Faculty are more effective in providing leadership on their own campuses if they have been exposed to a variety of perspectives, experiences, program ideas, and case histories offered by faculty from comparable institutions. Time and again, participating faculty singled out this exposure as a leading benefit of Project QUE participation. That cosmopolitan perspective is also enhanced by consultants with broad knowledge of programs and procedures in the immediate area of concern. The campus coordinator at one QUE college, for instance, advised colleagues at other colleges and universities to "make use of visits to other campuses as well as consultants in assembling information to bear upon the prospective program." Faculty also gain individual benefits (personal and professional development) from interinstitutional cooperation. The knowledge and skills that they gain can be of direct, immediate benefit to their students and institutions.

But how does an institution that is not invited to participate in a national project obtain these benefits? Institutions must make greater efforts (and even invest scarce financial resources) to develop cooperative arrangements and to seek assistance from colleagues at other colleges and universities to avoid "reinventing the wheel" and spending scarce time inefficiently. Visits by campus teams or planning committees to other campuses, invitations to knowledgeable colleagues to consult at one's institution, even the use of one-to-one and conference phone calls can be very beneficial to a program development process. Such efforts must not be abandoned during times of tight budgets.

Even the leaders of national projects can learn from each other. They often find their own hypotheses confirmed by the results of other projects with different types of institutions. For example, the Student Outcomes Project of the National Center for Higher Education Management Systems (NCHEMS), conducted between 1981 and 1983 with a diverse group of public institutions and supported by a W. K. Kellogg Foundation grant, identified five basic lessons learned, several of which sound very similar to conclusions reached in Project QUE (National Center for Higher Education Management Systems, 1983, pp. 6–8):

> 1. Information about student outcomes is generally available on campus if you look for it—but rarely in the form you want. [Project QUE does not have an exact parallel inasmuch as the NCHEMS Project dealt with the utilization of existing outcomes information, while QUE generated program-specific outcomes about which new information was produced.]
> 2. Address your . . . effort to a particular, commonly recognized issue or problem. . . . Participating institutions have been successful in their campus project largely to the degree to which they have maintained a sharp focus on a highly visible problem. [This lesson parallels Project QUE's concentration on a single program that was of special significance to the institution's mission and future.]
> 3. Involve as many kinds of people from as many parts of the campus as possible. . . . Form a coordination committee that includes representation from major campus constituencies. . . . [This lesson supports Project QUE's consultation and involvement principles and the use of a special campus team for program planning and development.]
> 4. . . . efforts are often positively influenced by external forces and individuals. [The Project QUE design made extensive use of workshops involving teams from several colleges to promote learning from each other and of outside consultants (both "professional" and peer) and project staff to influence program development. Of course, the entire Project was an "external force."]

5. When raising questions about student outcomes, be prepared for discussions to turn eventually to broad issues of institutional mission and
effectiveness. [Project QUE encouraged each participating institution to relate outcomes to institutional and student needs as defined by the mission
and major challenges facing the college.]

Perhaps one reason for the convergence of insights gained
from these diverse national projects points back to our initial
statement in this chapter: we have not so much learned new
things in this project as reconfirmed what we have all known
already to be the case. Both Project QUE and the NCHEMS
project have taught us once again that we know how to plan
effectively and how to effect systematic and consensually based
institutional change. This conclusion was also reached by many
leaders of Project QUE colleges. They knew what had to be done
even before the project began. QUE encouraged them to try
it out and learn from the process about their own institution
and its reactions to planned change: "I think the whole understanding of process is the most important piece of knowledge
gained [from Project Que]. We have knowledge of the importance of process in general and how it works or doesn't work
in the institution. We now know where some of the process problems are and hopefully we can overcome them in subsequent
efforts. I think it overrides all we learned about curricular development and student development theory, because all that knowledge is useless if it can't be implemented somehow. We had
intellectual agreement on the ideas proposed but had problems
when we attempted to implement them." As another project
coordinator suggested in more succinct terms: "Use the planning process. Trust it. It works."

Concluding Comments

Given that we seem to know what has to be done to effect systematic and successful academic change in our colleges
and universities, one wonders why this does not occur more fre-

quently. The real question becomes: Why do we seem to lack the courage, the vision, and the discipline to exert this type of leadership in our colleges and universities? The answer to this question may have much to say about the future role to be played by higher education in our changing society. Hopefully, Project QUE has helped sixty colleges find their own courage, vision, and discipline and through this book has helped to set the stage for other colleges and universities that are similarly in need of this form of leadership and an academic planning process to accompany it.

APPENDIX A
Project QUE Participants

Barry University
11300 N.E. 2nd Avenue
Miami Shores, FL 33161
Program Topic: Oral and written skills
Contact: Andre Cote, dean of the School of Arts and
Sciences

California Lutheran University
60 West Olsen Road
Thousand Oaks, CA 91360
Program Topic: Cluster/curriculum model to integrate
knowledge and improve student writing
skills
Contact: Lyle Murley, professor of English

College of Mt. St. Joseph
5701 Delhi Road
Mt. St. Joseph, OH 45051
Program Topic: Freshman course: reading, writing, listening, speaking skills
Contact: William C. Schutzius, associate professor of
humanities

College of Mt. St. Vincent
On-Hudson
Riverdale, NY 10471
Program Topic: International economics/business
Contact: Margaret Higgins, assistant professor of English

College of Notre Dame of Maryland
4701 No. Charles Street
Baltimore, MD 21210
Program Topic: Communications skills across the curriculum
Contact: Jeanne Stevenson, professor of history and
          political science

College of St. Teresa
Winona, MN 55987
Program Topic: A New Model for Liberal Learning:
          Design for Choicemakers
Contact: Susan Smith Batell, dean of academic affairs

Columbia Union College
7600 Flower Avenue
Takoma Park, MD 20012
Program Topic: Cooperative education
Contact: Anna Klimes, associate professor of education

Doane College
Crete, NE 68333
Program Topic: New mathematics skills component for
          Teaching Learning Center
Contact: Donald Ziegler, vice-president for academic affairs

Dominican College of Blauvelt
10 Western Highway
Orangeburg, NY 10962
Program Topic: Computer Information Systems Program
Contact: Philip Sciame

Edgewood College
855 Woodrow Street
Madison, WI 53711
Program Topic: General education: Foundations of Human
          Learning for Weekend Degree Students
Contact: Helen Dailey, coordinator of Weekend Degree
          Program

Eureka College
College Avenue
Eureka, IL 61530
Program Topic: Freshman studies
Contact: Rudolph Eichenberger, coordinator of Freshman
        Studies

Flaming Rainbow University
419 North Second Street
Stilwell, OK 74960
Program Topic: Upper division interdisciplinary cluster
        courses
Contact: Janet Milford Sanders, academic dean

Gardner-Webb College
P. O. Box 997
Boiling Springs, NC 28017
Program Topic: Program for the hearing impaired
Contact: Robert Morgan, professor of French and mathematics

Houghton College
Houghton, NY 14744
Program Topic: Recreation major
Contact: George R. Wells, professor of physical education

Huntingdon College
1500 East Fairview Avenue
Montgomery, AL 36194-6201
Program Topic: Honors program
Contact: Richard Anderson, head of Department of
        Language and Literature

Huntington College
2303 College Avenue
Huntington, IN 46750-9986
Program Topic: Revision of business and
        economics curriculum
Contact: Ann C. McPherren, assistant professor of business

Illinois Benedictine College
5700 College Road
Lisle, IL 60532
Program Topic: Scholars program
Contact: Phyllis M. Kittel, associate dean of faculty and
          instruction·

Illinois College
1101 West College Avenue
Jacksonville, IL 62650
Program Topic: Public service studies program
Contact: John L. Nies, vice-president for academic affairs

John Brown University
Siloam Springs, AR 72761
Program Topic: Planning for engineering accreditation
Contact: James V. Pearson, chairman of Division of
          Engineering

Kansas Wesleyan
Santa Fe at Claflin
Salina, KS 67401
Program Topic: Core studies program: Foundations for
          Decisions
Contact: Janet Juhnke, associate professor of English

The King's College
Briarcliff Manor, NY 10510
Program Topic: Field experience education
Contact: Carl G. Gustafson, chair of Division of Natural
          Science and Mathematics

King's College
133 North River Street
Wilkes-Barre, PA 18711
Program Topic: Career development
Contact: Donald W. Farmer, academic dean

Marian College
3200 Cold Spring Road
Indianapolis, IN 46222
Program Topic: Global studies/general education
Contact: Louis C. Gatto, president

Marion College
4201 South Washington
Marion, IN 46952
Program Topic: Multicultural activities
Contact: Bryon L. Tippey, chair of Division of Education
and Psychology

Mary College
Apple Creek Road
Bismarck, ND 58501
Program Topic: Freshman career development program
Contact: Charles Hanson, vice-president for student
development

Marylhurst Education Center,
College for Lifelong Learning
Marylhurst, OR 97036
Program Topic: New liberal arts major in human studies
Contact: Doug Robertson, program coordinator for social
studies

Marymount Manhattan College
221 E. 71st Street
New York, NY 10021
Program Topic: Implementation of a computer literacy
program
Contact: Barbara Rich, vice-president for student affairs

Mercy College of Detroit
8200 West Outer Drive
Detroit, MI 48219

Program Topic: General education—Contemporary
                citizenship
Contact: Jacqueline Zeff, dean of arts and sciences

Neumann College
Aston, PA 19014
Program Topic: Core curriculum
Contact: Sr. Margaret Patrice Gurley, OSF, vice-president
        for academic affairs

North Park College
3225 West Foster
Chicago, IL 60625
Program Topic: Internships
Contact: Peter Fellowes, acting dean of academic affairs,
        professor of English

Northland College
1411 Ellis Avenue
Ashland, WI 54806
Program Topic: Environmental studies
Contact: Kerry Burns

Notre Dame College of Ohio
4545 College Road
South Euclid, OH 44121
Program Topic: Project QUE
Contact: Mary Glennon, RSM

Oakland City College
Lucretia Street
Oakland City, IN 47660
Program Topic: General education
Contact: Presley W. Pendergrass, dean of academic affairs

Ohio Dominican College
1216 Sunbury Road
Columbus, OH 43219

Program Topic: Adaptation of core courses in humanities
                to weekend college
Contact: Sr. Ruth Caspar, professor of philosophy

Olivet College
Olivet, MI 49076
Program Topic: Integrate teaching of reading, writing,
                listening, and communication skills
                throughout the curriculum
Contact: Joel J. Epstein, professor and chair of the Depart-
        ment of History

Regis College
235 Wellesley Street
Weston, MA 02193
Program Topic: Integration of career services and intern-
                ship services
Contact: Edward Mulholland, director of freshman
        academic and academic grants

Roberts Wesleyan College
2301 Westside Drive
Rochester, NY 14624
Program Topic: Learning assistance across the curriculum
Contact: Elvera Berry

Rust College
1 Rust Avenue
Holly Springs, MS 38635
Program Topic: Competency-based approach to teaching
                and learning
Contact: Paul Lampley, academic dean

St. Andrews Presbyterian College
1700 Dogwood Mile
Laurinburg, NC 28352
Program Topic: Business/economics program
Contact: Robert J. Hopkins

St. Joseph's College
Rensselaer, IN 47978
Program Topic: Improve cognitive development in core
                curriculum
Contact: John D. Groppe, associate professor of English

St. Mary's Dominican College
7214 St. Charles Avenue
New Orleans, LA 70118
Program Topic: Development of upper division courses
                focusing on issues relevant to the world of
                the eighties and beyond

Seton Hill College
Greensburg, PA 15601
Program Topic: Core revitalization: An Integrative
                Developmental Approach
Contact: JoAnne Boyle, professor of English

Sioux Falls College
1501 S. Prairie Avenue
Sioux Falls, SD 57101
Program Topic: Business administration with a manage-
                ment emphasis
Contact: Allen Herrboldt, professor of business education

Spelman College
350 Spelman Lane, S.W.
Atlanta, GA 30314
Program Topic: Educational programs for adults
Contact: Pauline E. Drake, associate dean of continuing
                education

Thiel College
College Avenue
Greenville, PA 16125
Program Topic: Foundations for scientific thinking
Contact: Joyce Cuff, associate professor of biology

Tift College
Tift College Drive
Forsyth, GA 31029-2318
Program Topic: Business administration
Contact: Janet Woods, assistant professor of business
administration

Trevecca Nazarene College
333 Murfreesboro Road
Nashville, TN 37203
Program Topic: Marriage and family course
Contact: G. L. Pennington, director of workshops and
special programs

Trinity College
208 Colchester Avenue
Burlington, VT 05401
Program Topic: Freshman advising seminars
Contact: Janice E. Ryan, RSM, president

Westmont College
955 La Paz Road
Santa Barbara, CA 93108
Program Topic: Freshman year program
Contact: Edwin J. Potts, assistant to the president

William Jewell College
Liberty, MO 64068
Program Topic: Computer literacy
Contact: Jim E. Tanner, dean of the college

APPENDIX B
Expanded Case Studies
from Project QUE

College	Title	Authors
California Lutheran College Thousand Oaks, CA 91360	Clustering Courses: Project QUE at California Lutheran College	Lyle Murley
College of St. Teresa Winona, MN 55987	Design for Choicemakers: A Model Liberal Studies Program	Sr. Johanna Orlett Sr. Ingrid Peterson
Huntington College Huntington, IN 46750	Outcomes for Business: Project QUE At Huntington College	Robert B. Hale Ann McPherren
King's College Wilkes-Barre, PA 18711	Enhancing Careers: A Life Development/ Career Planning Program	Joan McGuiness Blewitt D. W. Farmer
Seton Hill College Greensburg, PA 15601	Necessary Combinations: Students, Outcomes and the Core Curriculum at Seton Hill College	JoAnne Boyle

Note: These case studies are available in an individual volume or as an appendix to William Bergquist and Jack Armstrong, *Planning for Quality: A Model for Effective Academic Program Development*, available from the Council of Independent Colleges, One Dupont Circle, Washington, D.C. 20036.

References

Argyris, C. *Intervention Theory and Method.* Reading, Mass.: Addison-Wesley, 1970.

Argyris, C., and Schön, D. A. *Theory in Practice: Increasing Professional Effectiveness.* San Francisco: Jossey-Bass, 1974.

Battaglini, D. "From the Idealistic to the Realistic." In J. Orlett (ed.), "College of Saint Teresa: Design for Choicemakers—a QUE Target Program—Final Report." Paper submitted to the Project QUE office, May 1, 1983.

Bergquist, W. H. "Responding to the Future Through Curricular Reform." *Liberal Education*, 1976, *62*, 229–244.

Bergquist, W. H., and Armstrong, J. *Quality Undergraduate Education: Project Work Manual.* Washington, D.C.: Council of Independent Colleges, 1979–1984.

Bergquist, W. H., and Armstrong, J. *Planning for Quality: Final Report to the W. K. Kellogg Foundation for Project QUE.* Washington, D.C.: Council of Independent Colleges, 1985.

Bergquist, W. H., Gould, R. A., and Greenberg, M. *Designing Undergraduate Education: A Systematic Guide.* San Francisco: Jossey-Bass, 1981.

Bergquist, W. H., Lounibos, J., and Langfitt, J. *The College 1 Experience: Integrating Work, Leisure and Service.* Washington, D.C.: Council of Independent Colleges, 1980.

Bergquist, W. H., and Phillips, S. R. *A Handbook for Faculty Development.* Vol. 1. Washington, D.C.: Council of Independent Colleges, 1975.

Bergquist, W. H., and Phillips, S. R. *A Handbook for Faculty Development.* Vol. 2. Washington, D.C.: Council of Independent Colleges, 1977.

Bergquist, W. H., and Phillips, S. R. *A Handbook for Faculty Development.* Vol. 3. Washington, D. C.: Council of Independent Colleges, 1981.

Boyle, J. "Seton Hill College: Planning, Developing, Testing, Evaluating the Target Academic Program—Core Curriculum Renewal—a Progress Report for Project QUE." Paper submitted to the Project QUE office, Oct. 11, 1982.

Boyle, J. "QUE Report: End-of-Project." Paper submitted to the Project QUE office, Aug. 30, 1983.

Briskin, A. "The Institutionalization of the Soul." Unpublished doctoral dissertation, the Wright Institute, Berkeley, Calif., June 1984.

Campbell, D. T., and Stanley, J. C. *Experimental and Quasi-Experimental Designs for Research.* Chicago: Rand McNally, 1966.

Caspar, R. "Project QUE: Phase III, Final Report: Ohio Dominican College, Columbus, Ohio." Paper submitted to the Project QUE office, Sept. 24, 1982.

Chickering, A., and others. *Developing the College Curriculum.* Washington, D. C.: Council of Independent Colleges, 1977.

Chickering, A. W., and Associates. *The Modern American College: Responding to the New Realities of Diverse Students and a Changing Society.* San Francisco: Jossey-Bass, 1981.

Cook, J. M. *Developing Learning Outcomes: Module 2 of a Handbook on Clarifying College Learning Outcomes.* Columbia, Md.: Council for the Advancement of Experiential Learning, 1978.

Cross, K. P. "Learner-Centered Reform." In D. W. Vermilye (ed.), *Learner-Centered Reform: Current Issues in Higher Education 1975.* San Francisco: Jossey-Bass, 1975.

Diamond, R., and others. *Instructional Development for Individualized Learning in Higher Education.* Englewood Cliffs, N.J.: Educational Technology, 1975.

Drake, P. "Spelman College Project QUE Phase III Progress Report." Paper submitted to the Project QUE office, 1982.

Eble, K. E. (ed.). *Improving Teaching Styles.* New Directions for Teaching and Learning, no. 1. San Francisco: Jossey-Bass, 1980.

Epstein, J. "TAP: Skills Program in Reading, Writing, Listening and Oral Communication." Paper submitted to the Project QUE office, Jan. 31, 1983.

Farmer, D. W. "Progress Report for Project QUE: King's College." Paper submitted to the Project QUE office, Feb. 18, 1981.

Foucault, M. *Discipline and Punishment*. New York: Vintage Books, 1977.

Gaff, J. G. (ed.). *Institutional Renewal Through the Improvement of Teaching*. New Directions for Higher Education, no. 24. San Francisco, Jossey-Bass, 1978.

Gaff, J. G. "Reconstructing General Education: Lessons from Project GEM." *Change*, 1981, *13*, 52–58.

Gaff, J. G. *General Education Today: A Critical Analysis of Controversies, Practices, and Reforms*. San Francisco: Jossey-Bass, 1983.

Greenberg, E., O'Donnell, K., and Bergquist, W. (eds.). *Educating Learners of All Ages*. New Directions for Higher Education, no. 29. San Francisco: Jossey-Bass, 1980.

Gustafson, C. G. "Phase III Progress Report." Paper submitted to the Project QUE office, June 1982.

Hale, R. "Project QUE: Final Report: Huntington College." Paper submitted to the Project QUE office, May 9, 1983.

Havelock, R., and others. *Planning for Innovation Through the Dissemination and Utilization of Scientific Knowledge*. Ann Arbor, Mich.: Institute for Social Research, 1971.

Higgins, M. "TAP Progress Report." Paper submitted to the Project QUE office, Sept. 20, 1982.

Huse, E. F. *Organization Development and Change*. St. Paul, Minn.: West, 1975.

Inhelder, B., and Piaget, J. *The Growth of Logical Thinking from Childhood to Adolescence*. New York: Basic Books, 1958.

Kelly, E. F., and others. *A Story of Essence: The Portrayal of a Science Curriculum*. Syracuse, N.Y.: Center for Instructional Development, Syracuse University, 1977.

Kepner, C. H., and Tregoe, B. B. *The Rational Manager*. New York: McGraw-Hill, 1965.

Kittel, P. M. "Illinois Benedictine College: Project QUE

1981–82 Report.'' Paper submitted to the Project QUE office, summer 1982.

Klimes, A. "The QUE Project (Cooperative Education): Columbia Union College." Paper submitted to the Project QUE office, June 21, 1983.

Knefelkamp, L., Widick, C., and Parker, C. A. (eds.). *Applying New Developmental Findings.* New Directions for Student Services, no. 4. San Francisco: Jossey-Bass, 1978.

Kolb, D. "Learning Styles and Disciplinary Differences." In A. W. Chickering and Associates, *The Modern American College: Responding to the New Realities of Diverse Students and a Changing Society.* San Francisco: Jossey-Bass, 1981.

Kolb, D. *Experiential Learning.* Englewood Cliffs, N.J.: Prentice-Hall, 1984.

Lindquist, J. (ed.). *Designing Teaching Improvement Programs.* Washington, D.C.: Council of Independent Colleges, 1978a.

Lindquist, J. *Strategies for Change.* Washington, D.C.: Council of Independent Colleges, 1978b.

Lindquist, J., and Tarule, J. "Evaluation Report: QUE Project, College of Notre Dame." Paper submitted to the College of Notre Dame, based on visit to college on May 11 and 12, 1982.

Lippitt, R., Watson, J., and Westley, B. *The Dynamics of Planned Change.* New York: Harcourt Brace Jovanovich, 1958.

McCoy, J. D. "Eureka College: Project QUE—Final Report." Paper submitted to the Project QUE office, May 27, 1983.

McKinney, T. E. "Faculty Development for Competency-Based Education: A Synopsis of the Current Status of the Quality Undergraduate Education Project." Paper submitted to the Project QUE office, May 1983.

McPeak, M. P. "Progress Report: 1981–1982." Paper submitted to the Project QUE office, Sept. 20, 1983.

Martorana, S. V., and Kuhns, E. *Managing Academic Change: Interactive Forces and Leadership in Higher Education.* San Francisco: Jossey-Bass, 1975.

More, H. T. "QUE Project Final Report: Notre Dame College of Ohio." Paper submitted to the Project QUE office, May 11, 1983a.

More, H. T. "Project QUE: Phase III Progress Report: Notre Dame College of Ohio." Paper submitted to the Project QUE office, Sept. 23, 1983b.

National Center for Higher Education Management Systems. "Institutional Uses of Student Outcomes Information: The NCHEMS/Kellogg Foundation Project." *NCHEMS Newsletter*, fall 1983, pp. 6–8.

Nelsen, W. C., and Siegel, M. E. *Effective Approaches to Faculty Development.* Washington, D. C.: Association of American Colleges, 1980.

Ogden, P. "Final Report—Project QUE: Roberts Wesleyan College." Paper submitted to the Project QUE office, May 23, 1983.

Palola, E., and others. "Program Effectiveness and Related Costs: An Overview." In E. Cavert (ed.), *Diversity by Design.* Lincoln: University of Nebraska Press, 1975.

Parker, C. A. (ed.). *Encouraging Development in College Students.* Minneapolis: University of Minnesota Press, 1978.

Peck, R. D. *Future Focusing: An Alternative to Long-Range Planning.* Washington, D.C.: Council of Independent Colleges, 1983.

Pendergrass, P. W. "Oakland City College—Project QUE." Paper submitted to the Project QUE office, Sept. 29, 1982.

Perry, W. *Forms of Intellectual and Ethical Development in the College Years.* New York: Holt, Rinehart & Winston, 1968.

Peters, T., and Waterman, R., Jr. *In Search of Excellence.* New York: Harper & Row, 1982.

Phillips, S. R., and Bergquist, W. H. "Solutions: A Guide to Better Problem-Solving." Unpublished manuscript, Intentional Management, Inc., Corvallis, Oregon, 1986.

Pilon, D., and Bergquist, W. *Consultation in Higher Education.* Washington, D.C.: Council of Independent Colleges, 1979.

Pirkl, M., and Orlett, J. "College of St. Teresa: Design for Choicemakers: A QUE Target Program: Final Report." Paper submitted to the Project QUE office, May 1, 1983.

Plunkett, L. and Hale, G. *The Proactive Manager.* New York: Wiley, 1982.

Rich, B. "QUE Final Report: Implementation of a Computer

Literacy Project at Marymount Manhattan College.'' Paper submitted to the Project QUE office, May 10, 1983.

Rodd, L. ''Project QUE End-of-Project Report.'' Paper submitted to the Project QUE office, Dec. 6, 1983.

Rogers, C. R. ''Toward a Modern Approach to Values: The Valuing Process in the Mature Person.'' *Journal of Abnormal and Social Psychology*, 1964, *668*, 160–170.

Rogers, E. M. *Communication of Innovations*. (3rd ed.) New York: Free Press, 1983.

St. Joseph's College. ''Final Report of Saint Joseph's College: QUE Project.'' Paper submitted to the Project QUE office, June 24, 1983.

Sanford, N. *Self and Society: Social Change and Individual Development*. New York: Atherton, 1966.

Sashkin, M., Morris, W. C., and Horst, L. ''A Comparison of Social and Organizational Change Models: Information Flow and Data Use Process.'' *Psychological Review*, 1973, *80*, 510–526.

Schein, E. H. *Process Consultation: Its Role in Organization Development*. Reading, Mass.: Addison-Wesley, 1969.

Schein, E. H. *Organizational Culture and Leadership: A Dynamic View*. San Francisco: Jossey-Bass, 1985.

Sennett, R. *Authority*. New York: Vintage Books, 1980.

Sprunger, B. E., and Bergquist, W. H. *Handbook for College Administration*. Washington, D.C.: Council of Independent Colleges, 1978.

West, R. ''End of Project Report: Marian College.'' Paper submitted to the Project QUE office, May 12, 1983.

Zaltman, G., Florio, D., and Sikorski, L. *Dynamic Educational Change*. New York: Free Press, 1977.

Index

211